PICCADILLY
THE HAY MARKET
PANTON STR.
JAMES STREET
NORRIS STR.
MARKET STR.
GREAT SUFFOLK STR.
L. SUFFOLK STR.
HEDGE LANE
St. Martins Church Yard
St. Martins in y. Fields
The Green Mews
THE ROYAL MEWS
Dunghill Mews
DURHAM YARD
GEORGE STR.
CRAVEN STREET
Hungerford Market
Timber Yard
JERMYN STREET
YORK STREET
Babmay's Mews
St. James's
CHARLES STREET
ST. ALBANS ST.
ST. JAMES'S SQUARE
PALL MALL
COCKSPUR ST.
CHARING CROSS
SPRING GARDEN
NEW STREET
Admiralty Office
Craggs Court
SCOTLAND YARD
MIDDLE SCOTLAND YARD
INNER SCOTLAND YARD
White Hall Stairs
WHITE HALL
Marlborough House
PARADE
Chapel
Privy Garden
Kings Arms Stairs
Treasury
Cock Pit
DOWNING STREET
AX YARD
CROWN COURT
CHARLES STREET
DUKE STREET
KING STREET
PARLIAMENT STREET
Manchester Stairs
ST. JAMES'S PARK
BRIDGE STREET
WESTMINSTER BRIDGE
UNION STR.
NEW PALACE YARD
QUEEN STREET
QUEENS SQ. PARK STR.
LONG DITCH
Cock Yard
THE BROAD SANCTUARY
Church Yard
St. Margaret
St. MARGARET'S STREET
Westminster Bridge Stairs
Stangate Stairs
THE BROAD WAY
TOTHILL STREET
PETTY FRANCE
St. PETER'S ABBY
OLD PALACE YARD
Great Almnery
DEANS YARD
GR. CHAPEL STR.
L. CHAPEL STREET
NEW TOTHILL STR.
Parliament Stairs
Timber Yard
BRIDGE STR.

The Buildings of Green Park

The Buildings of Green Park

A tour of certain buildings, monuments and other structures in Mayfair and St. James's

by **Andrew Jones**

ACC ART BOOKS

ISBN: 978-178884-116-0

First published by ACC Art Books in 2020
Reprinted (with corrections and additions) 2022

British Library Cataloguing-in-Publication Data
A catalogue record for this book is available from the British Library

The author and publisher gratefully acknowledge the permission granted to reproduce the copyright material in this book. Every effort has been made to trace copyright holders and to obtain their permission for the use of copyright material. The publisher apologises for any errors or omissions in the text and would be grateful if notified of any corrections that should be incorporated in future reprints or editions of this book.

Book design by Ned Campbell
Typeset in Enigma, Trilogy Sans and **Trilogy Egyptian**

MIX
Paper from responsible sources
FSC® C106600

Printed in Slovenia
for ACC Art Books Ltd., Woodbridge, Suffolk, UK
www.accartbooks.com

ACC ART BOOKS

→ Glass plate negative of Rysbrack's 1739 terracotta bust of Queen Caroline. Edward Kemp, c.1932

ENDPAPERS

Front: John Rocque, Plan of the Cities of London and Westminster and Borough of Southwark, with the contiguous buildings, 1746

Back: John Shury, Plan of London From Actual Survey, 1839

The endpapers show the profound changes that Mayfair and St James's underwent during the reigns of Kings George II–IV and William IV. In the map of 1746 (front endpapers), Mayfair is in large part undeveloped to the north of Curzon Street, Buckingham House is not yet Royal, Green Park extends to the south of Constitution Hill, St. James's Park is still a formal garden and, further afield, Belgravia does not exist.

By 1839 (back endpapers), Mayfair is more or less as we know it today, Buckingham Palace has been built and has absorbed a large piece of Green Park, St. James's Park has been remodelled by Nash into its current romantic form and Belgravia developed.

To the memory of Queen Caroline of Ansbach (1683–1737), indisputable Queen of Green Park

E. Dayes del.

VIEW of the QUEEN'S WALK,

in the Green Park.

Contents

← Dayes's *View of the Queen's Walk*, 1797. The reservoir was filled in the 19TH century

vodafone UK
15:06
64%
MAYFAIRBUILDINGS
Posts
mayfairbuildings
Green Park
Liked by matthewjrose and 52 others
mayfairbuildings 47: Apsley House: until 1771, this plot contained the Hyde Park Lodge, a collapsing apple stall and the Hercules' Pillar inn. The... more

Foreword

IT IS HARD TO OVERESTIMATE the philosophical wisdom behind Andrew Jones's project. We hear – and tell ourselves – so much about the importance of living in the present, of being grateful, of opening our eyes to the beauty of what is most immediately around. Andrew has been able to put these bromides into practice, to make them his – and by extension our – living reality.

What is especially touching, though Andrew is far too modest to do anything but briefly allude to this, is the contrast between the project at hand and Andrew's customary interests. It is easy to describe someone as internationally minded or a citizen of the world. Andrew truly is those things and many more: he has a prodigiously well-stocked mind and heart. Those of us who follow his Instagram feed and know him outside of pandemics have always been awed by the breadth of his travels and the properly global nature of his sympathies. He has an intimate knowledge of sub-Saharan Africa and a great appreciation of the culture of many of its countries and regions. He is especially alive to modernism in African architecture – and is sensitive and knowledgeable about pretty much all the arts of all major cultures.

The pandemic was therefore likely to pose Andrew with a special challenge, for how could such a vagabond mind cope with being restricted to such a narrow geographical and cultural domain? The answer is in our hands. Like other great minds forced into seclusion by external circumstances, his spirit broadened even as his liberty of movement closed. The French philosopher Pascal warned us that all of man's unhappiness stems from our inability to stay alone in our room. Andrew was forced to be – metaphorically – alone in his room; and he learnt just what to do. He was able to see the world in a grain of sand, as the Buddhists say every sage should be able.

His peregrinations around central London are at one level about architecture, about recovering the forgotten history of so much we have all seen without for that matter properly noticing. But it is far more than this – which is why the text is so poignant. We are learning about London and also, beneath the surface, receiving a lesson in appreciation, in the art of looking properly around us in search of what is beautiful, habitable, heart-warming and consoling.

One day (we are still in the pandemic as I write), the world will reopen. One day, Andrew will be back in the Democratic Republic of the Congo or the Ivory Coast. But what this book provides a legacy to is his edifying ability to open himself up to experience, to lay his own ego aside and to find delight and interest in what we normally rush by.

This is at one level a book about a part of London and its buildings. At another, it's a book about learning to savour our lives – while there is still time.

Alain de Botton
London, June 2020

Preface

WHEN THE LOCKDOWN was imposed in March 2020, I realised, like most of us, that I would have to change my habits quickly in order to manage the sudden restrictions on my movements. For years I had been travelling to faraway places three or four times a month and spending my weekends in galleries, auction houses and museums or visiting buildings in distant cities.

And then all that suddenly stopped.

Now, I am fortunate to live in a historic part of London, on Piccadilly overlooking Green Park. And I was even more fortunate not to fall ill (or to have family fall ill) during this time. On the first day of the Lockdown, I resolved that I would spend what would normally be my commuting time walking in the park as my permitted daily dose of exercise.

I had always been conscious of the better known buildings in the neighbourhood: Spencer House, Lasdun's 26 St. James's Place, The Ritz and its William Kent annex. But, on my first walk of the Lockdown, I started to see just how many interesting buildings there were, both architecturally and, with a little reading, historically. And as I warmed to my subject, I realised that even the æsthetically less interesting buildings had the most varied history.

And so I set about researching and writing about one building a day. As long as it was clearly facing the park (or had at some point faced the park – as is the case with Apsley House or Marble Arch), it would qualify. Since moving here 15 years ago I had assembled a small collection of books about the neighbourhood and, as every public library was closed, these, together with the web, were my sources.

I posted my daily building on Instagram and soon found myself in interesting dialogue with various followers. Had I seen this building? Did I know about a particular association of that building? I once had a job interview there etc. I would typically post early in the morning before work, having finished my research and pictures the night before, and then the dialogue would start as followers would comment.

For 48 days I documented every building on Green Park starting with Lancaster House and moving anti-clockwise up the Queen's Walk, along Piccadilly to Hyde Park Corner and down Constitution Hill, ending at Buckingham Palace. And then on Day 48, I realised that I was having such fun that I embarked on a series of monuments and structures of Green Park, working my way back and clockwise, until I had completed these also.

The Lockdown started at the end of winter and continued into Spring. The photographs I took reflect this – the trees are wintry to begin with and bursting with luscious green foliage by the end. Looking back, I could not have photographed the front of many of these buildings in the same way had the Lockdown started later (or had I gone clockwise). There was also practically no traffic, the days were sunny and the air remarkably fresh.

In this book I have published my Instagram posts with minimal editing. Each piece is, therefore, limited to around 2,200 characters and the photographs are almost all taken with my smartphone. The research is limited to the resources I had available at the time.

I hope you enjoy this book, both as a guide to this wonderful pocket of London and as a memento of the strange confinement brought about by COVID-19.

ANDREW JONES
London, June 2020

↑ Piccadilly Turnpike (artist unknown), c.1790: the entrance to London, with the Adam Brothers' Apsley House **[47]** on the left

Acknowledgements

THIS BOOK BEGAN its life on Instagram and I am deeply grateful to my friends and followers for their insights, contributions and encouragement. The regular comments and DMs I received from John Austin (in which he also shared Philippa Barton's extraordinary knowledge of historical British buildings) should really be included in the Bibliography, so valuable and interesting were they. Other notable Insta-contributors included Nina Campbell, Hutton Wilkinson, Tom Naylor and Nell Lyhne, whose offerings spanned everything from personal memories and flying freeholds to the very existence of The Pantheon. I was also touched by the many messages of encouragement I received throughout the process from friends and strangers alike around the world – among these, Manfred Flynn Kuhnert's really did stand out. All of this provided a surprisingly lively and interesting social life during Lockdown and made me value social media like never before.

As the idea of turning my posts into a book began to form, I received invaluable advice from Felicity Rubinstein, Nicky Dunne of Hayward Hill books in London and Nick Higbee of the Pallant House Gallery Bookshop in Chichester. This advice led me to my publisher, James Smith – I am grateful to him for his excellent guidance, and to his colleagues at ACC Art Books, in particular Susannah Hecht, for all their support and professionalism in producing this book.

While preparing the text and the images for publication, I turned to friends and neighbours and was delighted by their generosity in giving me introductions as well as access to resources and buildings for photography. I would like to single out: Molly Lowell Borthwick; Bernard Donoghue; Justin Pinchbeck and Anders Winum of the Sheraton Grand Hotel; Simon Alexander and 'Piccadilly' Jim at the Athenæum Hotel; David Cowdery and the staff at The Cavalry and Guards Club; Trevor Dunmore of the Royal Automobile Club; Wing Commander Paula Wilmot of The Royal Air Force Club; Jackie McDevitt at The Ritz; Peggy Fogelman of the Isabella Stewart Gardner Museum; Jules Shellabear and Victor Keegan of The Thorney Island Society; Polly Bielecka of Pangolin London; Anne Fitzpatrick; May Geolot at Daniel Crouch Rare Books; and Caroline Townshend and Letty Cornwell of the Eaton Square Senior School.

I am very grateful to Alain de Botton for his wonderful Foreword. Reading it, I felt like Le Bourgeois Gentilhomme in his philosophy class, surprised and charmed to learn that he had been speaking prose all his life.

To convert a series of posts into a manuscript is a surprisingly big job. Sarah Boxell supported me magnificently as did Gabrielle Quinn with her exacting proof reading of my text.

It has been a huge pleasure to work with my wonderful friend and designer Ned Campbell. His taste, inventiveness, wit, intellectual engagement and rigour made the design process hugely enjoyable.

Finally, particular thanks to Laura Hodgson, my wife, who for several months indulged my need to talk about little else other than the subject matter of this book, has given me wonderful editorial and æsthetic counsel throughout and who took the beautiful photograph of 26 St. James's Place and Spencer House for the cover. — *AAJ*

Buildings, Monuments and Structures

Map of Green Park

Key to locations

The Queen's Walk c.1925 seen from the roof of the newly completed Devonshire House **[19]**. Wimborne House **[16]** is on the left

[PART I]

Buildings of Green Park

1

Lancaster House 1825–41

'I HAVE COME from my House to your Palace,' exclaimed Queen Victoria as the Duchess of Sutherland welcomed her to what was then Stafford House. This truly is the grandest mansion in St. James's, if not in London. Seeing its Bath stone façade glowing in the early morning sunshine became one of the great pleasures of my daily outing during Lockdown.

Designed by Benjamin Dean Wyatt and Philip Wyatt for George IV's brother, the Duke of York, construction of York House started in 1825. The building replaced Queen Caroline's Library [62] as well as the late 17TH century Godolphin House. The interior of the house was unfinished when the Duke died in 1827.

The house was bought by the Government for use by The Royal Society, but then sold shortly thereafter to the 'Leviathan of Wealth', the 2ND Marquess of Stafford (later Duke of Sutherland). (The £72,000 purchase price was used by the Government to create Victoria Park in Hackney.) Stafford engaged Robert Smirke to add the top floor. This was Smirke's second involvement with this house; his original designs for a simpler York House had been rejected by the Duke of York's mistress, Elizabeth Manners, Duchess of Rutland. The name of the building was changed from York House to Stafford House. The interiors were finished by the Wyatts and added to by Smirke and later (1839–41) Charles Barry, the architect of Bridgewater House [5] and are in an elegant Louis XIV style (also used by the Wyatts at Apsley House [47]).

The Sutherland household became famous for its liberal gatherings and in 1848 Frédéric Chopin played in the presence of Queen Victoria and Prince Albert. The house stayed in the Sutherland family until 1912 when it was bought by soap baron Sir William Lever, who renamed it Lancaster House (after his native county) and presented it to the nation for use by the London Museum. Since the end of World War II it has been used by the Foreign and Commonwealth Office for conferences and official events – as such, it played an important role in the decolonisation process: the agreements for the independence of Malaya (1957; now Malaysia) and Rhodesia (1980; now Zimbabwe) were concluded here. In 1962, the Franco-British agreement for the development of Concorde was signed here and, in 2015, it was also the venue of a luncheon I attended on the occasion of the Chinese State visit.

The building has, since 1922, housed the 39,000 bottles of the Government Wine Cellar.

← Glowing Bath stone, early in the morning

↓ An early plan of the principal floor of York House, c.1825

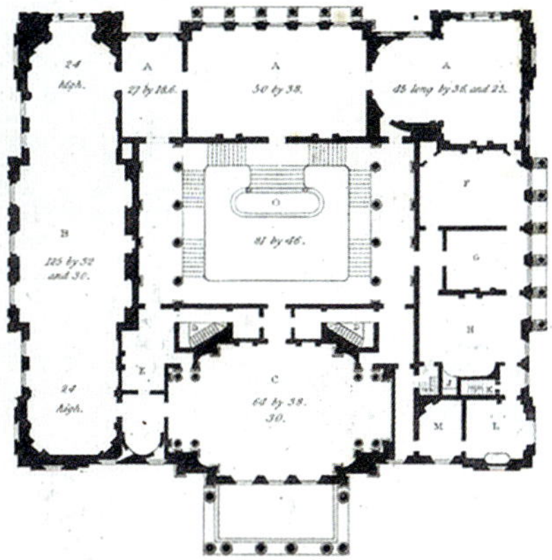

↑ Unity and Concorde: the 1962 treaty is signed

→ Revolutionary moment: Mugabe signs the Lancaster House Agreement, 1979

2 Warwick House 1770–1

IF THERE is one recurring occupation of the inhabitants of Green Park, it appears to be that of the media mogul. We begin with Rothermeres, but will also encounter Beaverbrooks [3], Murdochs [9], Barclays [17] and Borthwicks [43].

Originally designed by Sir William Chambers for Mr and Mrs Errington (1770–1), Northumbrian landowners, this house replaced a group of smaller old buildings. The Erringtons had the house decorated by Giovanni Battista Cipriani with scenes from Herculaneum, which are thought to have survived until 1894. The Earl of Warwick bought the house in 1853 making numerous changes and it was 'French Renaissanced' in the late 19TH century.

Since 1924, the house has belonged to the Rothermere newspaper family. In the late 1940s and early '50s, the Viscountess Rothermere (née Anne Charteris) hosted famous parties attended by young artists such as Lucien Freud and Francis Bacon (who once booed Princess Margaret off stage when she attempted to sing a Cole Porter song at one such party). Lady Rothermere, who had long been in a sadomasochistic relationship with James Bond creator Ian Fleming, divorced the 2ND Viscount Rothermere in 1951 to marry Fleming. Towards the end of the 20TH century, the house was occupied by Ambrose Congreve. In his 1993 diary, James Lees-Milne describes how Congreve lived "*en prince*" and marvels at how "the *luxe* of Warwick House is for these days astounding".

When first built, the house was contiguous to Queen Caroline's Library [62] until the Library's demolition in 1825 to make way for York (now Lancaster) House [1]. At that time, Milkmaid's Passage was created – so named because of the numerous cows kept (under licence from the Home Secretary) in the park throughout the 17TH–19TH centuries, from whose udders warm milk could be bought as shown in the picture by Benjamin West.

The house can only be accessed through the Stable Yard of St. James's Palace.

→ French Renaissance flourishes

↓→ Milkmaids and customers were a regular presence in Green Park and St James's Park from the 17TH–19TH centuries, as shown in this picture by Benjamin West, c.1801. Westminster Abbey is in the distance

↑ Lady O'Neill, later to become Lady Rothermere. Photograph by Bassano, c.1937

3

Stornaway House 1794–6

STORNAWAY HOUSE was designed by Samuel Wyatt (1794–6) for Lord Grenville (then Secretary of State for Foreign Affairs and later Prime Minister of the Ministry of All the Talents). When Lord Grenville left the house in 1800, it was taken over by the playwright, politician and gunpowder manufacturer Miles Peter Andrews, who used the house to entertain on a lavish scale. Other occupants have included John George Lambton (later the 1ST Earl of Durham), an important actor in the Reform Bill, and the Canadian newspaper proprietor, Lord Beaverbrook.

The bow front follows the original line and the rather outsized pediment was added to the side in the 19TH century. The house was partially destroyed during World War II and the bombed-out shell turned into offices in the late 1950s; it now accommodates Cheyne Capital.

→ The north façade with its statement pediment

'I can hardly keep wondering at my own folly in thinking it worthwhile to leave my books and garden, even for one day's attendance in the House of Commons.'

—LORD GRENVILLE

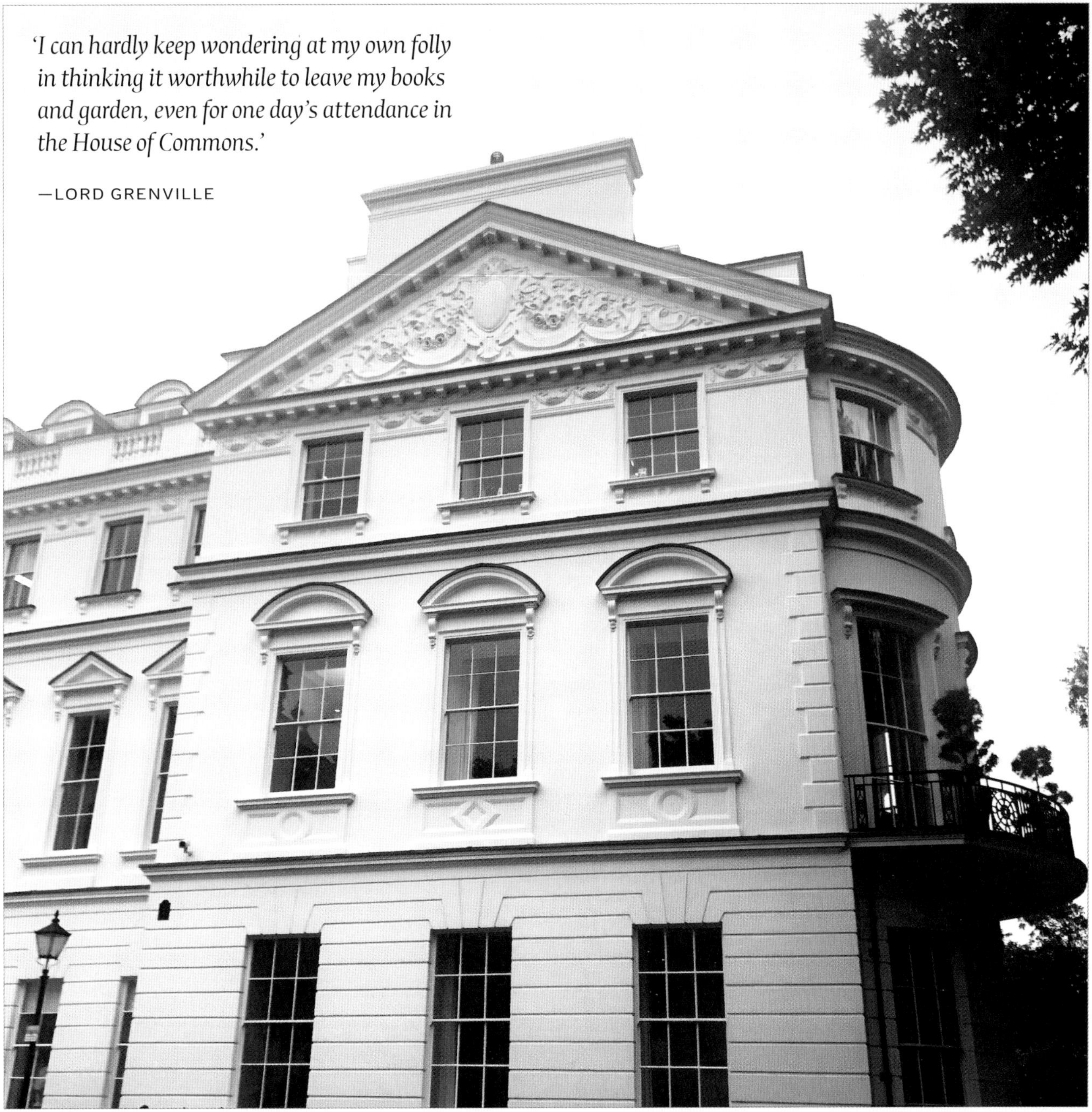

4 Selwyn House 1904

THE CURIOUSLY stranded Selwyn House was built by Norman Shaw in 1904, although in early Victorian style. It replaced a building part of which had, like Bridgewater House [S], been designed by Charles Barry.

The current building was damaged during World War II and refurbished by Pilkington Glass in 1949 and again in the 1960s for use as its headquarters with stylish interiors by Kenneth Cheesman. During the 1949 renovations, a hidden safe was discovered by workmen behind a panel under a staircase. It contained diamond earrings and gold pencils, as well as a packet of faded telegrams. One of these telegrams had come from Cecil Rhodes and had been written during the Siege of Kimberley during the Second Boer War.

It is now a private house again, owned by Rusudan Makhashvili, the Georgian 'MedSwiss' medical centre entrepreneur.

→ The mid-century elegance of the Pilkington Glass headquarters, 1960s

←↑ A neo-Romantic view of Selwyn House and St James's Palace, late 1940s; the east façade's Edwardian appearance today

↑ The refreshingly rugged south side

5

Bridgewater House 1845–8

Now owned by the Latsis shipping family, the magnificent Bridgewater House is in my view the most glamorous house in London and was, almost inevitably, the setting for Grantham House, the London residence of the Crawleys in *Downton Abbey*, as well as for Marchmain House in the 1981 television mini-series of *Brideshead Revisited*.

The house is by Charles Barry (1845–48), who also designed the Houses of Parliament and the nearby 'Florentine' stretch of Pall Mall comprising the Travellers' Club and the Reform Club. The Bridgewater Italian palazzo is even grander than his Reform Club, adorned with urns and chimneys and other decoration and fronted by the most elegant garden (also designed by Barry). At the back are separate doorbells for 'Groom' and 'Coachman'.

Bridgewater House is the most recent of several grand houses on this site. The first of these, Berkshire House, was built around 1626–7 for Thomas Howard, who had been created Earl of Berkshire by Charles I (to whom, when Prince of Wales, he had been Master of the Horse) and who declared himself for The King during the Civil War. Berkshire House was occupied by the Portuguese Ambassador in 1654 and by the French Ambassador in 1665. There are contemporaneous references to 45 chimneys having to be swept.

In 1668, Charles II bought Berkshire House for his mistress, Barbara Villiers, Countess of Castlemaine (who was, in 1670, to become the 1st Duchess of Cleveland), reputedly the most powerful of Charles II's mistresses, and known as 'The Uncrowned Queen'. It is said that a tunnel linked what then became Cleveland House to St. James's Palace.

The current building was commissioned by Francis, 1st Earl of Ellesmere. Via his father, he had inherited the magnificent collection of France Egerton, 3rd Duke of Bridgewater, valued at the time at £150,000 and comprising works by Caracci, Luini, Poussin, Raphael, Romano, Titian, Veronese etc. from the Orléans Collection, for which a large gallery was built. Twenty-five pieces of the collection are now in the National Gallery, with others in the National Gallery of Scotland and Castle Howard.

←↙ Formal entrance on Cleveland Row

↓ The supremely elegant garden, also by Barry

↑ Doorbells at the back entrance in Little St James's Street

6

4 Catherine Wheel Yard 1950

It is surprising to find this pocket of 1950s suburbia tucked in-between two exceedingly grand neighbours, Bridgewater House [5] and Spencer House [7]. It is set back a little, but still with a park view, and is therefore very much a Building of Green Park.

The neo-Georgian terrace, of which this is the end house, was built in 1950 following World War II bomb damage in what was then the mews of Spencer House. It was designed by W. Curtis Green & Sons, architect of Stratton House [20] and of the Wolseley restaurant.

It is one of the very few houses on Green Park, along with the William Kent House (now part of The Ritz [17]), that is entirely of brick without being clad in limestone or plastered. Closer inspection reveals fine brick coursework – an elegant rhythm of three stretchers for every header – as well as a handsome escutcheon incorporating the Spencer cypher. Its address comes from the Catherine Wheel Tavern (once on this site).

Charming in its incongruity!

←↑ Keeping up with the Bridgewaters with the use of an Italianate balustrade

→ Elegant coursework and a handsome escutcheon

7 Spencer House 1756–8

All I can say whenever I see Spencer House is 'Hurrah!'

Spencer House is such a joyously flamboyant and quirky building. Its façade is dominated by a huge pediment, which generously spans five of its seven bays (compared to the usual much stricter 2:3:2 formula on, say, Albany in Piccadilly), and is bedecked with palm fronds, statues of Bacchus, Ceres and Flora (by Michael Henry Spang) and a quantity of urns.

Spencer House was built for John and Georgiana Spencer by John Vardy the Elder (1756–8) and then James 'Athenian' Stuart, who also designed the neo-classical rooms on the first floor, some of the first of their kind in 18TH-century Europe. In the 1780s–90s Henry Holland executed further refinements to the interior and, in the 1840s, Philip Hardwick decorated the ground floor and restored the first floor.

The house has always belonged to the Spencer family, with a variety of tenants during the 20TH century, including the 9TH Duke of Marlborough and his wife (*née* Consuelo Vanderbilt), the Ladies' Army and Navy Club, Christie's and the Economist Intelligence Unit. Lord Jacob Rothschild, under a long lease from the Spencer family, undertook a 10-year scholarly restoration programme in the 1980s–90s to return the house to its condition after Holland's alterations of the 1780s–90s. As part of this restoration, the garden was returned to its 1795 layout by Todd Longstaffe-Gowan.

It is now a lovely museum and the most beautiful place for a party.

When you reach the Pantheon **[64]** look back and admire how Spencer House's façade inadvertently forms its portico.

↓ Bacchus, Ceres and Flora at dawn

→ The relatively modest entrance on St James's Place, opposite № 26 **[8]**

8 26 St. James's Place 1959–60

'The architect's job is to give a client not what he wants but what he never dreamed that he wanted; and when he gets it, he recognizes it as something he wanted all the time.'

—SIR DENYS LASDUN

THIS IS Denys Lasdun's modernist dream of 1959–60. The distinctive 3:2 rhythm on the parkside façade articulates the very modernist split-level apartments inside this veritable *millefeuille* of duplexity! Flats have a grand 1½-height drawing room with the other rooms laid out on single-height floors (as can be seen on the St. James's Place side).

What is so brilliant about this building in this setting is the constant æsthetic banter with Spencer House and its other neighbours. Look at how the giant proportions of the 1½-height floors tie into the grand proportions of the façade of Spencer House. The much more modest St. James's Place façade is in harmony with its less monumental neighbours, while the side façade echoes the bays on the main elevation of Spencer House. The restrained front door nods to its neighbour's at Spencer House and the concrete roof feature on the side plays with the open pediment on the south side of Spencer House.

There have been houses on this site since the late 17TH century. The predecessor house, a heavily Victorianised 18TH-century construction, was destroyed by bombing in World War II. Occupants of this had included politicians, Richard Rigby ('bon vivant of the first order, and a statesman of the second') and 'Jubilee Dicky' (Richard Vernon MP).

So, so good!

← In dialogue with Spencer House

↑ The entrance on St James's Place

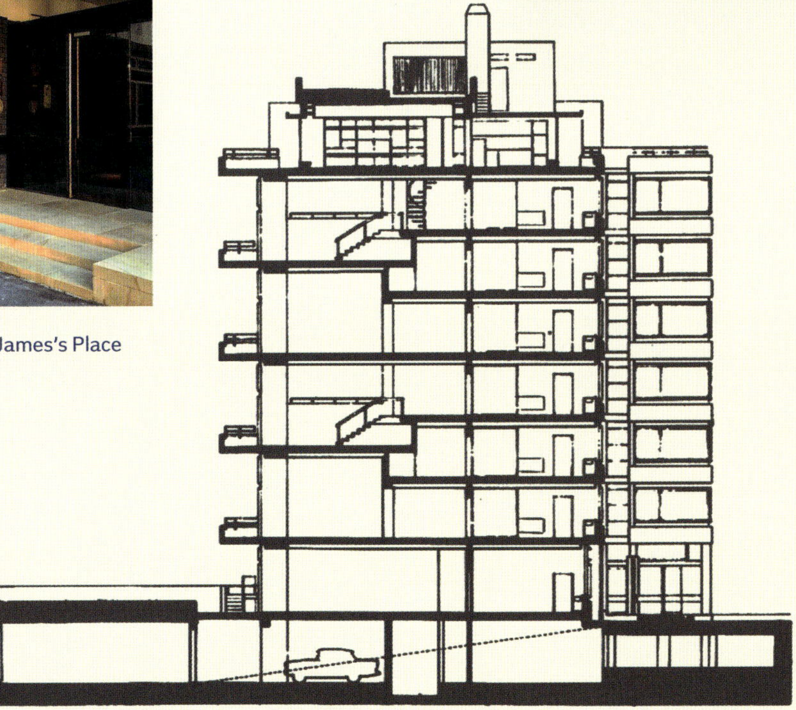

↑← Duplexes and grand drawing rooms stacked high

9

25 St. James's Place 1960s

25 ST. JAMES'S PLACE built by Vigers & Co. in the early 1960s, replaced a Regency house documented by Sir John Soane and destroyed during World War II.

Houses have stood on this site since 1699. The second house was built by Lady Hervey around 1749, to her own designs (with the help of Henry Flitcroft) and with the intention of making it 'look as [much like] the country as I can', 'contrary to all Palladian rules'.

The house was occupied from 1816–1844 by Sir Francis Burdett, the reformist politician known as 'Old Glory' and father of philanthropist Baroness Burdett-Coutts [see 20].

It currently contains the London home of media magnate Rupert Murdoch.

↑ Mary Lepel, Lady Hervey, c.1762, was not partial to Neoclassicism

↑ Old Glory, the energetic Sir Francis Burdett

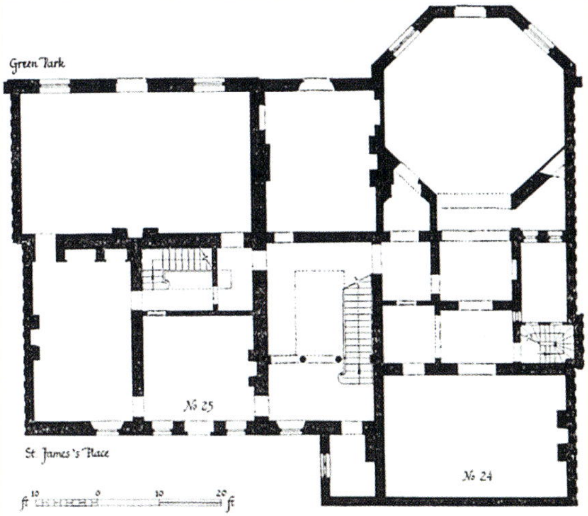

← 24 and 25 St. James's Place were once a single home

10

24 St. James's Place *1960s*

'If I were not the Earl of Guildford, I should have liked to be a librarian.'

—FREDERICK NORTH

A SLIVER OF a building I rather like, from the mid-1960s, with an intriguing rhythm on its short ribbon-windowed façade: 1:2:1:2:1:1:2, presumably to accommodate the duplexes inside. And, round the back, a lovely travertine entrance with rather nice typeface.

The house's predecessor is just visible in a 1797 print by Edward Dayes as a two-storey house with an octagonal library [see also the plan in **9**]. It is also visible next to 23 St. James's Place shortly before demolition [**11**].

From 1816–25 Frederick North, 5TH Earl of Guildford, Governor of Ceylon (1798–1805), notable philhellene, Eastern Orthodox convert, and founder of the Ionian Academy (Ionios Akidamia) on Corfu, the first university in modern Greece, lived here. Guildford has been described as 'not merely a bibliophile but a bibliomane'. His library at 24 St. James's Place was lined in snakewood he had brought back from Ceylon and his collection is now in the British Library.

← № 24 is just to the right of the tree where the octagonal library can be seen *(see pages 6–7 for full image)*

→ Frederick North, later 5TH Earl of Guilford, in Rome, 1790

↓ Travertine with gilded lettering at the entrance

11 23 St. James's Place 1929–30

THE 'very last big private house built in the West End' (Pevsner), 23 St. James's Place was built for James A. de Rothschild by Simpson & Ayrton (1929–30), who also designed 4 Millbank (the grand neo-classical building near Smith Square) and the old Wembley football stadium. The Regency-style bow windows of the park front would have matched those of its neighbours when the house was built, including those at 24 St. James's Place [10] before it was redeveloped.

James A. de Rothschild was part of the French branch of the Rothschild family and came to England from Paris after he unexpectedly inherited Waddesdon Manor from his great-aunt, Alice de Rothschild (1847–1922). While no great collector himself, he inherited a third of his father's significant picture collection and brought it to Waddesdon. He also commissioned Leon Bakst to paint a *Sleeping Beauty* series; this was initially installed at 23 St. James's Place but later moved to Waddesdon.

The house replaced an early 19TH-century house that had been built by John Lubbock and occupied by the Lubbock family for much of the 19TH century.

↓ St James's Place entrance [inset: James A. de Rothschild, c.1920]

→ One of seven panels by Bakst, *The Prince Discovers the Princess and Wakes Her with a Kiss,* shows de Rothschild as the Prince

12 Castlemaine House, 21-22 St. James's Place

1958–60

A RATHER CHEERY Disneyesque neo-Regency sort of a block, with a stylish entrance, by Maurice Bebb. (Maurice Bebb was also involved in the Smithsons' glorious Economist Building nearby on St. James's Street. As consultant to Robert McAlpine, it was his idea to include three blocks on that site.)

While the site was being excavated in 1956, an 'ice pit' of c.1670 was found. The pit had been filled with clay, brick rubble and ash, as well as pieces of late 17TH-century Delft and German stoneware. Commissioned by the Duchess of Cleveland [5], this ice pit would have been filled with snow and ice in winter and used for cooling drinks in summer. There were five other ice pits in Green Park, but hers was the only non-Royal one – most fitting for the 'Uncrowned Queen'.

Various houses have stood on this site since the 17TH century, with the current structure replacing two houses that had been badly damaged during World War II. An earlier incarnation of № 21 belonged to Lord Moira; the house was surveyed by Sir John Soane.

An eminent inhabitant of № 22, from 1803 to 1855, was Samuel Rogers, author of *The Pleasures of Memory*. His house was designed by James Wyatt with cornices and chimney pieces by John Flaxman. Rogers was a man of extraordinary taste: Lord Byron spoke of his 'almost fastidious elegance' and his collection spanned Etruscan vases and Old Master drawings; the Christie's auction of his collection on his death lasted 22 days. Baron von Bunsen, in his memoirs, describes 'a delightful dinner party at Rogers's [...], all quite in the style of a rich Roman in the time of Augustus – original drawings of Raphael, etc., after dinner, vases before. The beautiful Titians etc., of the dining-room ingeniously lighted so that the table alone was in the shade'. Guests at Rogers's famous breakfasts and dinners included Madame de Staël, Sheridan, Sydney Smith, Walter Scott, J.M.W. Turner, Wordsworth and Washington Irving.

'He [...] had the kindest heart and the unkindest tongue of any one I ever knew,' said Fanny Kemble.

← Samuel Rogers's house

↓ Neighbourly reflections in the 1950s entrance

↑ The ice pit discovered, 1956

→ An artist's impression of Maurice Bebb's scheme for the building

↑ Samuel Rogers, c.1850

13 The Royal Over-Seas League 1734–40, 1906–8

I HAVE VERY fond memories of staying at The Royal Over-Seas League as a young boy with my mother during the Winter of Discontent (1978–79). I think this must have been my first night in London. My bedroom overlooked Green Park, then covered in snow. In contrast to the rest of the country, I was Content.

The Royal Over-Seas League was founded in 1910 by Sir Evelyn Wrench to cater for that 'far flung brotherhood of individual men and women of diverse creeds and races living under differing conditions in different latitudes'. An apt description of the young Me, wrenched from home on Lake Geneva en route to a Victorian boarding school in Hampshire.

The left hand portion of the building (four bays in brick) on this, the park side, is Rutland House by James Gibbs (1734–40) for Mary, Dowager Duchess of Norfolk. The Palladian/Regency stone side is Edwardian by Ambrose Poynton Jun. (1906–8). There is also a 1930s block by Messrs Joseph on the entrance side in Park Place. The old gatehouse to Rutland House in Arlington Street is well worth going to see.

In 1851, a hot-air balloon crashed into this building.

One of the last members of the Rutland family to occupy this house was the artist Violet Manners, Duchess of Rutland (mother of Lady Diana Cooper and grandmother of John Julius Norwich). During World War I, the Duchess converted Rutland House into a hospital, with Lady Diana Cooper serving as a nurse at the house.

→ The hot-air balloon crash of 1851

↓ Violet Manners, Duchess of Rutland

↑ The Winter of Discontent, Piccadilly Circus

→ The old gatehouse to Rutland House in Arlington Street

14 Arlington House 1934–6

I HAVE ALWAYS found Arlington House to be rather glamorous, not least because it contained my favourite local restaurant, *Le Caprice,* one of London's great institutions and impeccably run by Jesus Adorno, which very sadly never reopened after Lockdown.

Built in 1934–6 by Michael Rosenauer (who went on to build the Time & Life building and the Westbury Hotel on Bond and Conduit Streets), and clad in travertine and Portland stone, it replaced four grand houses. These included the only major 18TH-century London Gothic house, Pomfret Castle, built by the Countess of Pomfret (1757–1761) during her widowhood, and derided by her neighbour Horace Walpole, opposite. The other house of note was 19 Arlington Street, an 18TH-century house remodelled by Robert Adam (and with furniture by Adam and Thomas Chippendale), the setting for Johann Zoffany's painting *Sir Lawrence Dundas and his Grandson*.

Arlington House reputedly has a rather fabulous penthouse with a retractable roof, as featured in a disturbing film, *The Look of Love,* about Paul Raymond of Raymond Revuebar fame, which I once watched on a 'plane somewhere over Algeria.

↓ The main entrance in Arlington Street with one's beloved Le Caprice (R.I.P.) at bottom left

→↘ London Gothic: Pomfret House, 1757–61

← Johann Zoffany: *Sir Lawrence Dundas and his Grandson*, 1775

15

21 Arlington Street *1738*

THE SECOND Earl of Sefton (1772–1838; aka 'Lord Dashalong' on account of his fast four-horse driving through the streets of London), once inhabited this house, where he is said to have given magnificent dinners. The dinners were prepared by Louis Eustache Ude, once *chef d'hôtel* to Madame Mère (Napoléon's mother) having been apprenticed in Louis XVI's kitchens in Versailles (where his father was a cook) and at the time Britain's most famous chef and author of *La Science de Gueule* ('sauces are the soul of cookery ... seasoning is in cookery what chords are in music'). Ude is said to have resigned from working for the Earl of Sefton because one of the Earl's guests had added pepper to his soup. He later worked for the Duke of York, upon whose death Ude is said to have exclaimed: 'Ah, *mon pauvre Duc;* how much you will miss me when you are gone.'

The house is curiously set back from the park, with a rather charming shabby-chic country-garden entrance and an elegant Ionic porch on the main façade (and a truly terrible Edwardian mansard and late 20TH-century front courtyard). It was designed by Giacomo Leoni in 1738 for the 2ND Viscount Shannon and then altered by William Chambers in 1769 for Viscount Weymouth and again in the 19TH and 20TH centuries.

In 1948 it was adapted for offices and now features on the *Offshoreleaks* website.

↑ Louis Eustache Ude

The garden path

16 William Kent House *1740–50*

ANOTHER HURRAH moment as we come to William Kent (aka Wimborne) House, built by Kent in two phases (1740–50) for Henry Pelham who used this, rather than 10 Downing Street, as his Prime Ministerial quarters and who subsequently commissioned Kent to design the Horse Guards Building in Whitehall, the architect's greatest building. William Kent House is such an elegant and understated, and yet very grand, building (Pevsner talks of its 'casual asymmetry').

The house has changed names over the years with its owners: each of its three Ducal occupiers (Grafton, Beaufort and Hamilton) renamed it and, in the 1880s, it was named Wimborne House when ironworks millionaire Sir Ivor Guest was further ennobled, becoming the 1ST Baron Wimborne.

Under the next generation, in the 1930s, the house became famous for its chamber music concerts hosted by the beautiful Lady Wimborne (who took the young composer, William Walton, 20 years her junior, as her lover).

In 2000, the house was annexed by The Ritz allowing guests to glide, a little confused (at least I always am), from 18TH-century France to 18TH-century England and a series of rather magnificent (if rather overwhelmingly restored) Kent party rooms. This ends a century-long saga: The Ritz had first tried to buy the house in the early 20TH century only to be rebuffed by Lord Wimborne, who replied that he was thinking of enlarging his garden and asked: 'how much do you want for The Ritz?'.

← The young William Kent, c.1710–20, by William Aikman

↓ Alice Wimborne, c.1914

→ Dinner overlooking the Park

17

The Ritz Hotel 1903–7

AND SO we reach the end of the Queen's Walk and its apogee, one's beloved Ritz: a little piece of the arcade in the rue de Rivoli and a large dollop of the court of Louis XVI, miraculously landed on Piccadilly, with almost non-stop *crêpes suzette* within, an eternal flame for Margaret Thatcher who died here on 8 April 2013 after being generously accommodated by the Barclay brothers, then the owners of the hotel.

This is one of César Ritz's four original Ritz hotels (along with Paris, Madrid and Barcelona) and was designed by Charles Mewès (who also did Paris and Madrid) and Arthur Davis in 1903–7. The Ritz stands on a site soaked in hotel history – for years the Old White Horse Cellar coaching inn stood here and, in the 20 years prior to the Ritz being built, the Walsingham House and Bath Hotels occupied this plot.

It has an unusually strong structure due to building regulations not having caught up with technology: it is the first large steel-framed building in London but also (at the insistence of the local building authority) supported by its cladding system. This perhaps explains how it survived several bombs during World War II.

The hotel is filled with benign ghosts such as that of the exiled King Zog of Albania (with whom a distant relative of mine once eloped) and his entourage of 30, including his right-hand man, Monsieur Martini, who weekly would settle the royal tab in gold; that of the train enthusiast King Boris of Bulgaria, who, having spent the night riding on the footplate of a train, arrived at The Ritz black with soot only to be directed to the coal chute; and, of course, the ghost of Evelyn Waugh, who would lunch on caviar, grouse and peaches.

Staying here has always been delightful and I shall never forget my stag party in the Trafalgar Suite:

Children of the Ritz
Sleek and civilized
Frightfully surprised
We know just how we want our quails done
And then we go and have our nails done

—NOËL COWARD

↑ An early picture postcard of the hotel. The wall of the old Devonshire House **[19]** is visible to the left along with the old Berkeley Hotel **[18]**

↑ Walsingham House was built in 1888 at a cost of £140,000 but by 1903 had been replaced by The Ritz

↓ In need of a Martini: King Zog retreats to The Ritz after Italy had annexed Albania

↑ Mewès and Davis's supremely elegant lobby

18

70-73 Piccadilly 1970–4

PEEPING OUT from behind The Ritz into Green Park is 70-73 Piccadilly by Chapman Taylor Partners.

It is a building I have always found very pleasing, not least because for many years the Iran Air office displayed a model Concorde in the window (three Concordes were ordered by the Shah on the eve of the revolution but cancelled by the killjoy Ayatollah [another casualty of the revolution was the Shah's glorious cellar]). The promotional models were proudly retained and I once (unsuccessfully) tried to convince the local representative to sell me the one on Piccadilly.

There used also to be a rather lovely sculpture of a man on a horse by Elisabeth Frink in the little forecourt in front of the rather less lovely retro-sleazy Mayfair Club ('London's most exclusive gentlemen's club' according to one website); that statue has now been moved to the forecourt of the Ralph Lauren building on Old Bond Street.

Behind this building, in the same block, is the (recently closed) Holiday Inn hotel, reminding us that hotels have stood on this site for centuries: first (in the 18TH century) the Gloster Coffee House and Hotel. Rebuilt as the St. James's Hotel, in 1897 it became the Berkeley Hotel, which moved to its Knightsbridge premises when the current building was erected in 1972.

The building (together with the hotel behind it) is currently being redeveloped. Mercifully, a rather thumping David Adjaye scheme that had been approved has been dropped and now it seems that the existing building with its very satisfying grid and bevelled windows will be kept. A little part of me hopes that the Iran Air Concorde could be returning to Piccadilly.

↑ Iran Air office, late 20TH century

↑ Chapman Taylor's perfect grid with a thoughtfully placed K2 phonebox

↑ The Mayfair Club before demolition in 2020

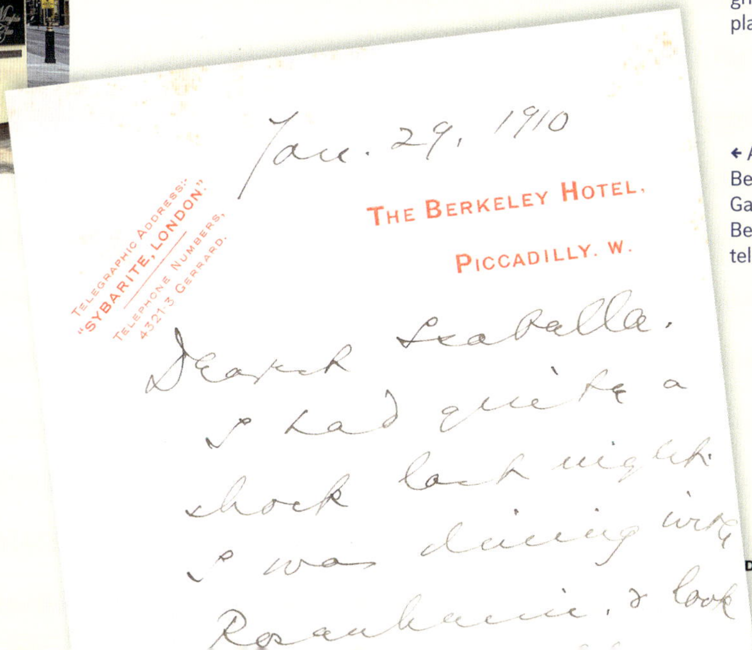
Jan. 29, 1910

THE BERKELEY HOTEL,
PICCADILLY. W.

TELEGRAPHIC ADDRESS: "SYBARITE, LONDON."
TELEPHONE NUMBERS, 4321 3 GERRARD.

Dearest Isabella.
I had quite a shock last night. I was dining with Rosenheim, & look

← A letter from Bernard Berenson to Isabella Stewart Gardner written from the old Berkeley Hotel – note the telegraphic address

19

Devonshire House 1924–6

IF THE Ritz [17], opposite, is an elegant slice of Paris and Versailles, then Devonshire House (1924–6) is a delicious scoop of New York. It could, with the addition of a tower or two, be an apartment building on Central Park West and was in fact designed by an American architect, Thomas Hastings of Carrère and Hastings, the architect of Henry Clay Frick's mansion on Fifth Avenue (now the Frick Collection) and also of the New York Public Library.

It replaced the Duke of Devonshire's palace designed by William Kent and later James Wyatt and Decimus Burton (the gates to which are further down Piccadilly [25] and the wine cellars of which became the ticket office for Green Park Underground Station [59]). The plan of the old Devonshire House was, essentially, that of a country house transposed to London: a practical, pillared, everyday ground floor and a sweeping double staircase (replaced by Decimus Burton with the famed white marble staircase with its glass handrail) taking visitors upstairs to a more formal part of the house for entertainment, including one of the first known formal dining rooms. The picture collection was extraordinary (in contrast to that at Chatsworth at the time, which mostly consisted of family portraits). Many of its interiors remain in storage at Chatsworth.

Built as apartments and now converted into offices, it displays beautiful 'sparing but gay Cinquecento ornament' (Pevsner) and lovely bronze detailing around the shops (originally dominated by Citroën and Rootes showrooms) and the tube station.

This must be M&S's most elegant setting (even if the retailer hasn't really risen to the Cinquecento challenge – imagine a refrigerated *cassone* for the display of ready-made curries).

→ 'Sparing but gay Cinquecento ornament'

↑ Devonshire House, c.1800, behind its high wall

→ The ballroom of the old Devonshire House in the late 1800s, with its wonderful William Kent fireplace

↑ Mr Albert Levy's drawing room by Oliver Hill as published in *Country Life* in 1927

20 Stratton House 1929

BUILT IN 1929 by W. Curtis Green & Sons, who had designed the Wolseley car showroom (now restaurant) in 1922 and went on to design the Dorchester Hotel (1931).

It is a dapper if dull building, which replaced an 18TH-century house with a ceiling by Robert Adam that had belonged to the Coutts family from 1795 until it was demolished in 1929 (although towards the end it had, like so many buildings on Piccadilly at the time, become a club).

For years it was occupied by the immensely rich, extravagant and generous Mrs Coutts, widow of Thomas Coutts the banker. Originally an actress (Miss Harriet Mellon), she was, by the time of her death in 1837, the Duchess of St. Albans. She left her (then colossal) £1.8 million fortune (which if it had been converted into gold would have required 107 men to carry it, assuming each man could carry 298lbs) to her step-granddaughter Baroness Burdett-Coutts (daughter of Sir Francis Burdett [9]), who became a famous philanthropist and whose white cockatoo hung in the dining room window overlooking Green Park fascinating generations of passers-by.

In the 1930s, the building contained the MG showroom. Between 1940 and 1945 it housed the Government of The Netherlands in exile.

W. Curtis Green & Sons' building was refurbished in 2010 and a 12,000 sq. foot/1,100 sq. metre penthouse added with its own entrance on Stratton Street. On the ground floor in Stratton Street is the legendary *Langan's Brasserie,* a magnet for artists in the late 1970s. It used to have a wonderful collection (sadly sold at Christie's a few years ago), including a wraparound Patrick Procktor mural of Venice in its upstairs room – but in 2020 was in need of (urgent) refreshment.

↑ The old Stratton House, c.1900

DECORATION OF THE BARONESS BURDETT-COUTTS' HOUSE
80, Piccadilly

↑ Party time, 1887

→ The MG showroom, 1930s

21

81 Piccadilly 1920s

A MYSTERIOUS BUILDING but rather a lovely one: small and almost an afterthought next to the stately (and relatively pompous) Stratton House.

It has some very pretty details, especially the corner 'ship's prow' (perhaps a nod to the fact that The Royal Thames Yacht Club once stood here), and a nice Art Deco front on Bolton Street. Almost Viennese.

Two important facts:

1] what is now Pret a Manger used to be the Libyan Arab Airlines office in the days of Col. Gaddafi (*Prêt-à-Tuer*) – the old logo remained on the door for years;

2] it is on the site of the famous Watier's club, founded by the Prince Regent during a dinner party at which members of Brooks's and White's were complaining about having to eat endless boiled fowl in oyster sauce. This prompted the Prince Regent to instruct Watier, his French chef (who had escaped France during the Revolution), to take a house and start a dining club.

The club only lasted 15 years and the gambling there – especially games of 'Macao' – bankrupted most of its members. George 'Beau' Brummell was made perpetual president of the club, which was affectionately also known as the Dandy Club.

'Brummell's idea of dress was never extravagant, rather it was a sort of finished simplicity – "exquisite propriety" was Byron's phrase for it – and his leading maxim, "fresh linen and plenty of it" might be commended to the sternest of rationalists.' (Stern)

↑ The corner building of the late 19TH-century. Walsingham House, the predecessor building to The Ritz **[17]** is visible to the right and the walls of the old Bath House **[22]** to the left

→ The wonderfully fanciful corner detailing

↑ Fresh linen and plenty of it: Beau Brummell

22

82-84 Piccadilly – Clarges Mayfair 2014–17

Everything was 'hugely overdone: wealth-wealth-wealth was screamed aloud wherever one turned,' wrote Beatrice Webb about a dinner at Bath House in 1906. This plot has a long history of extraordinary wealth, with a brief 50-year interlude of incongruous practicality.

Built by the Pulteney family in 1740 as the Pulteney Hotel and replaced in 1821 for banker Alexander Baring, 1st Baron Ashburton, inhabited by railway baron Baron de Hirsch in the late 19th century and South African diamond magnate Sir Julius Wernher in the early 20th century and then by his widow Lady Ludlow (who in the 1930s had Serge Chermayeff redecorate a drawing room in the modernist style) – the house here 'might appropriately be re-christened "the Millionaire's Home"' (Dasent).

The Regency Bath House was demolished in 1958 to build Reed House (by Lewis Solomon, Kaye & Partners), which housed first Martins Bank and then the Qualifications and Curriculum Authority as well as, reputedly, MI5. Working purposes such as these are an aberration for this most extravagant of plots.

But, in 2014–7, a new development, Clarges Mayfair (by Squire & Partners) – the newest building on Piccadilly – managed to restore the intrinsic sense of money associated with this block with the erection of 34 flats with a 25-metre pool, a fully staffed spa and a new drive and *porte cochère* at the rear (just like Bath House once had) and achieving Mayfair's highest ever price per square foot. The penthouse flat has the scale of a decent country house with a grand staircase across three floors.

So we are well and truly back to the grandeur of the 19th century. The building is in safe and unimaginative international contemporary style but it works well (and has attracted some much needed local amenities such as a gleaming Porsche showroom on the ground floor and the wonderful Comptoir and Deli Robuchon) and its monumentality matches that of its neighbours to the east.

The development also includes new premises for the Kennel Club offering 'dog owners and those working with dogs an unparalleled source of education, experience and advice on puppy buying, dog health, dog training and dog breeding'. What more could one ask for?

↓ The Regency Bath House in 1958

↑ 84 Piccadilly, c.1960, showing the old Kennel Club to its left

← Martins Bank, Reed House, c.1964

↓ Ashburton Place, the newest street in Mayfair, serves as the driveway

↑ Seen from the corner of Clarges Street, the building has commanding views over Green Park

23

85 Piccadilly/47 Clarges Street 1966

THIS USED to be the Duke of Grafton's house ('New Grafton House'), built by the 3RD Duke to the designs of Robert Taylor and completed in 1779. From the late 17TH to the early 18TH century, before Clarges Street was built, this had been Clarges House, serving a spell as the Venetian Embassy. In 1875 it was adapted by John Norton for the Turf Club (which at one point had 16 Dukes among its members) in 'ornate free Renaissance' style.

New Grafton House was demolished in 1966 and replaced with a building designed by Clifford Culpin & Partners, mixing flats and commercial usage but curiously retaining a sliver of the old building on Clarges Street in-between it and Charles James Fox's old house next door (with the horizontal banding apparently broken where there was once a drain pipe).

The commercial parts of the current building were originally intended as a car showroom (perpetuating the tradition of Piccadilly car showrooms started by the original Wolseley and recently revived by Porsche next door [22]) over three floors (linked by a car lift which also serves the residents' car park), but became the Lebanese Fakhreldine restaurant (designed by Lucas Mellinger). This change of use meant that, for years, residents parking their cars who pressed the wrong button in the car lift would end up in the kitchen of the restaurant to the bemusement of both residents and falafel-rolling kitchen staff.

The restaurant is now called Hide with chef Ollie Dabbous producing excellent Michelin-starred takeaways during the Lockdown (under the brand Hide at Home). There was also once a nightclub in the basement called Tokyo Joe's. In 1990, a gunman took hostage the 75 patrons of the nightclub, bizarrely asking for a 'plane for him and most of the other patrons (which included Kuwaiti royals) to take him, and them, to Beirut (presumably to carry on partying). Andrew Grima, the jeweller, lived here in the 1970s. Now a zebra looks out onto Green Park from one of its windows.

← Clarges House in the 17TH century

↑ The Turf Club shortly before redevelopment in the 1960s

↑ The current building retains the line of the Turf Club

← A sliver of Grafton House remains on Clarges Street

24

86/89 Piccadilly & 2/3 Half Moon Street *1950s*

James Boswell, Lola Montès, Bertie Wooster, Algernon Moncrieff in *The Importance of Being Earnest,* Bulldog Drummond, Lord Berners and Wilfred Owen have all at various times lived on Half Moon Street. It is also the current home of my parents. The street was named after the Half Moon Tavern, which stood on what is now 86/89 Piccadilly.

Sir Walter Scott warmly describes his meeting with the elderly Fanny Burney (Madame D'Arblay) when she lived in the building (which was then a linen drapers' shop) and there are descriptions of it around 1914 as having also been a 'brush warehouse'.

The lovely 1950s reliefs on the end of the Half Moon Street façade are by Harold J. Dow (who was a contender for the Diana Fountain [60]) and, in 1958, Coventry firm W. S. Hattrell & Partners designed a Jaguar showroom, which now houses Essie, the carpet shop (and was also once a Libyan Arab Airlines office – how many premises did they have on Piccadilly?).

The building also has a rather magical address for the mathematically minded: 2/3 ½ Moon Street, or 0.33 recurring...

↑ Fanny Burney, c.1784

← Harold J. Dow's relief panels

↓ Jaguar showroom, late 1950s/early 1960s, with a gleaming Mark 2

← A sliver of N°s 86/89 around 1890 is visible on the far right, opposite Green Park Chambers **[26]**

25 Devonshire Gates 1735

TOGETHER WITH the ticket office at Green Park tube station (housed in what used to be the Duke of Devonshire's wine cellar [see 59]), the Devonshire Gates are all that is left of the old Devonshire House [see 19].

The gates were moved here, at the upper end of the Broad Walk, in 1921, when the house was demolished. The ironwork has been attributed to Jean Montigny, a Huguenot craftsman.

While one of the oldest structures on Piccadilly, the gates are in fact a relative newcomer, having been commissioned for a house in Turnham Green in 1735 and then bought for Chiswick House in 1837 (when the Cavendish coat of arms was added), only arriving in Piccadilly in 1897 as a friendly replacement for the tall wooden gates set in the deeply unpopular, high walls around Devonshire House (these 17TH-century walls were a remnant of the previous house designed by Hugh May for Lord Berkeley on the site of Hay Hill Farm).

The crest on the gates bears the punning Cavendish motto, *'Cavendo Tutus'* or 'Safe by Caution'. The beautiful vermiculated 19TH-century piers with their Greek-key band follow Lord Burlington's design for Chiswick. The lead sphinxes are 18TH century. The bicycle lock, which keeps them firmly, permanently and inexplicably closed, is thought to be late 20TH century, in its original plastic sheath.

↓ An Egyptian moment in Mayfair

↑ The gates were once the entrance to Devonshire House **[19]**, 1890s

→ A resident of Piccadilly

→ The view towards The Ritz **[17]** from the courtyard of the old Devonshire House **[19]**

26 Green Park Chambers 1883

AN OLD eccentric on Piccadilly – the only brick building overlooking Green Park – this building was designed by J.G.F. Noyes in 1883. For many years, Half Moon Street was a street of bachelor pads and *pieds-à-terre* that attracted all manner of literary figures [*see also* **24**]. Green Park Chambers, with its park frontage, was the luxurious tip of this bachelor iceberg.

Lots of high Victorian detail to enjoy, from the red and white voussoirs over the shop fronts, to the dates and dolphins on the plasterwork and the flamboyant Flemish baroque gables. It is currently being redeveloped into six grand apartments as part of the refurbishment of Cambridge House [27].

From 1919 to 1997 it was the bedroom wing of the Naval and Military Club [27] and then lay derelict for over 20 years.

The Chambers have a lovely view into Green Park down the Broad Walk to the glittering gold of the Victoria Memorial in front of Buckingham Palace – a sort of axis of Victoriana.

↑ When the restoration is complete the view across the Park will take in the Victoria Memorial

27 Cambridge House 1756–8

CAMBRIDGE HOUSE (also known as Egremont House, Cholmondeley House and 'In and Out House' [for its lettered piers]) is almost an *hôtel particulier* – set back from Piccadilly in a courtyard – and a rare remaining 18TH-century house on this stretch of the street.

A huge plot, with an interior garden originally designed by Capability Brown, it was built in 1756–8 by Matthew Brettingham (who was also working on Holkham Hall in Norfolk and used craftsmen from there for this London project) for the 2ND Earl of Egremont, who died here in 1763 'of an apoplexy, which from his figure was reasonably to be expected', according to Lord Chesterfield. The house was then inhabited by the Marquess of Cholmondeley who, in 1814, hosted a ball there for the allied victors including Czar Alexander of Russia [see also 63]. Later, the Duke of Cambridge (George III's seventh son) occupied the house and died here in 1850. In a curious incident a few days earlier, while leaving the house in her *barouche*, Queen Victoria had been attacked with a cane by a former officer of the 10TH Hussars, Robert Pate, and sustained injuries to her forehead.

In 1850 Lord Palmerston,

> *'The frolicsome statesman, the man of the day*
> *A laughing philosopher, gallant and gay'*
> (*Piccadilly*, Frederick Locker-Lampson)

bought the house from the Duke of Cambridge's estate.

When Palmerston died, there was talk of building the Catholic Cathedral of London here, but in the end the house was bought by the Naval and Military Club, which stayed here until 1997. It has passed through various developers' hands since, falling into terrible disrepair, but is now being turned into an hotel by the Reuben brothers. The portico (a Victorian addition) has been temporarily removed so there could be no worse time to photograph this otherwise very lovely building (apart from in World War II).

← The In and Out Club, c.1895

↓ Bomb damage, November 1940

↓ Witty anarchists

28 95 Piccadilly 1886

WHAT APPEARS at first to be a pale Victorian emoji in its currently covered state is in fact a graceful Franco-Flemish townhouse by Alfred Lovejoy (1886) that housed the American Club from its foundation (over a lunch at The Savoy) in 1918 until the 1980s when its lease expired.

Anthony Lejeune noted in his book *The Gentlemen's Clubs of London* (1979) that 'the disappointing thing, to an English visitor, about the American Club is that it contains so little which is specifically American'. But there is one exciting fact about the American Club: in Alfred Hitchcock's (wonderful) *Foreign Correspondent* (1940), Johnny Jones (no relation) intends to lunch there but is instead lured to Westminster Cathedral where he narrowly avoids being murdered. And the baddy in that film is called Mr Krug (no doubt an associate of King Zog's Monsieur Martini [see 17]).

The previous building on this site belonged to another John Jones (again no relation), an extremely successful but very modest military tailor whose collection of 18TH-century French furniture forms the basis of the Victoria & Albert Museum's collection of that period – there is still a dedicated display to his generous bequest. This wonderful clock (below) is one of 16 clocks he gave to what was then the South Kensington Museum.

The house is now part of the Cambridge/Egremont House hotel development after plans to reconvert the building into a large family home were reversed (presumably due to lack of John – or any other – Jones with £70 million to spare).

↑ Resplendently Franco-Flemish, 1885, photographed by Bedford Lemere

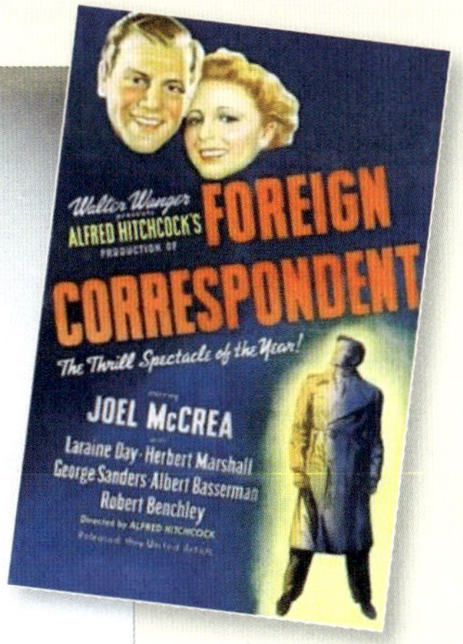

← In Hitchcock's film, Johnny Jones misses a lunch date and narrowly averts disaster

←↓ Dapper John Jones's exquisite collection formed the basis of a generous bequest to the future V&A

29 100 (96) Piccadilly 1891

Looking out from the windows of 96 Piccadilly are several Soviet spies and soldiers, part of film director Ilya Khrzhanovsky's 'staged reality experience' DAU in which the life of Soviet physicist Lev Landau is dramatized across several decades of Communist Russia in 'the Institute', a disused swimming pool in Kharkiv, N.E. Ukraine and also in 96 Piccadilly, S.W. Mayfair (appropriately Sovietised). (The BFI website has a trailer for the project and the *London Review of Books* an amusing article.)

The house began life in the 17TH century as the White Horse Tavern (which gives its name to the side street). Before this part of Piccadilly became fashionable in the mid-18TH century, sculptors and stone masons had their workshops along the street and this was Carter's Statuary Yard [*see also* **57**]. There have been various houses on the site and Sir Walter Scott stayed here several times between 1809–1820.

The current building is by T. & F.T. Verity (1891) and is rather elegant and restrained in design, if somewhat garishly clad in yellow Ham Hill stone among its soberly be-Portlanded neighbours – a lone Edam in a sea of Burrata – and was built to house the short-lived Junior Travellers' Club (a Victorian equivalent of an Unaccompanied Minor?) before housing the Junior Naval and Military Club, aka 'The Incubator'. It underwent an extensive conversion in the 1980s: it was combined with the building next door [30] to become a mixed apartment and office building and was also renumbered 100 Piccadilly.

In the 1950s the building housed the supremely elegant '96' restaurant of which the young Egon Ronay was general manager and which the then Princess Elizabeth frequented. Ronay describes how he 'would receive *Tout Londres* in its lounge and instantly decide whom to sit at which table – an important judgement only to those who did not matter. This was called the art of 'dressing the room''.

↑ The Junior Travellers' Club shortly after contruction, 1892, photographed by Bedford Lemere

→ The supremely elegant '96', frequented by Princess Elizabeth

↑ A Soviet spy peers out over Piccadilly

30

100 Piccadilly 1883

What is now an apartment building hidden behind a narrow façade, was, a very long time ago, the Duke of Beaufort's house before becoming, in 1875, the Badminton Club (named after the Duke's country seat), one of several clubs in London dedicated to coaching (aka 'four-in-hand' or the sport of driving a stage coach with four horses), in this case with stabling for 50 horses at the back. The Club built the present structure (designed by R. Edis) in 1883 – with some very pretty stone carvings outside, one of which bears the architect's signature.

The main feature of the building, apart from its extensive stables, was a glass-domed 'flower court', accessed from Piccadilly through a curious tunnel-like corridor. The court is still there but in a very 1980s idiom.

As driving coaches fell out of fashion, the club disbanded in 1938 and the building was taken over by the Public Schools Club, which stayed here until 1972 when it merged with the East India Club in St. James's Square – a club increasingly short of eligible members given that the East India Company had been dissolved 98 years earlier. The history of the Public Schools Club is filled with heroic efforts to modernise itself without, it seems, the realisation that its very brand might undermine those attempts – a sort of vegetarian meatloaf in clubland: first, a separate women's wing was built in place of the stables and, in the 1960s, the club decided to open its membership to people who had not been to a public school (this time, without a separate wing). When it finally closed in 1972, not having been successful in these various attempts at modernisation, 'regrettably there were even two fruit machines, one in the main club, the other in the ladies' annex' (Anthony Lejeune). Reassuringly, however, the club's smoking room was, until the very end, regarded as a 'comfortable halfway house between a school common room and clubland'.

In the 1980s, the building was turned into apartments, with three fully furnished show apartments by David Hicks.

← The playfully floral stonework around the doorways on Piccadilly, includes the architect's signature

↓ A portcullis, heraldic badge of the house of Beaufort, crowns the building

↑ The entrance tunnel leading to the flower court

31 Japanese Embassy 1890–2

THIS COLOSSUS, like its modest neighbour at No 100, is by R. Edis (1890–2). The juxtaposition of the two buildings makes them a Victorian version of Charles Barry's Travellers'/Reform Club parade in Pall Mall, 50 years before – but, rather than recreating a Florentine Renaissance street, Edis presents us with a jagged neo-Elizabethan procession.

The present structure replaced four town houses (No 102 once belonged to Thomas Lawrence; and No 103, the Hamiltons, with Nelson to stay) and was built for the Junior Constitutional Club, founded in 1887, one of numerous Conservative clubs in London during the 19TH century. The popularity of political clubs such as this among 19TH-century urban middle-class men was extraordinary. Within three years of opening the club had over 10,000 members, though that number had already halved by 1900 and it closed in 1904.

The next tenant was also politically aligned – the pro-tariff reform United Empire Club – and probably just as dull as its predecessor. I suppose Mar-a-Lago must also have a pro-tariff/protectionist whiff, but an enthusiasm for trade barriers as the main criterion for membership of a club does seem obsessive. A virtual United Empire Club still exists online. Its website asks: 'Can you imagine mingling ... with business successes, celebrities, politicians, nobility and even royalty?' It goes on optimistically to proclaim that some members hold 'English Titles ... bringing with them heritage of a bygone era when a nobleman or woman was by nature NOBLE, and gentlemen were GENTLE in nature, FAIR, HONOURABLE and DECENT' (pity all those women lacking such upper case attributes).

The building was the first marble-faced building in London and I have never warmed to it. In 1989, it was converted for use by the Japanese Embassy, a late work of Chamberlin, Powell, Bon & Woods, architects of the Barbican. It is a great relief that there is now a sensible occupant such as the Japanese Embassy, after the legions of pro-tariff lunatics of the past, even if the peacefulness of the neighbourhood is occasionally disturbed by anti-whaling demonstrations.

But imagine how wonderful it would be to replace this insipid structure with a gleaming new one by Kengo Kuma.

→ Still hanging on: the monogram of the Junior Constitutional Club

↓ A little light relief among the neo-Elizabethan *lourdeur*

↑ The crisp door plate of the Embassy

32 105 Piccadilly 1850–1

JAN VAN NOST, the 18TH-century sculptor, had his workshop here before, in 1788, Michael Novosielski built a house for the 7TH Earl of Barrymore (with a later porch by Robert Smirke). The Prince Regent's sobriquet for Barrymore was 'Hellgate', along with 'Cripplegate' for his club-footed brother, 'Newgate' for his youngest brother, and 'Billingsgate' for his foul-mouthed sister. Such was the owner's propensity for gambling that the bailiffs, who were permanently on hand, would dress in his livery and serve at his dinner table.

The house was then acquired by the 3RD Marquess of Hertford (the original for Thackeray's Marquess of Steyne in *Vanity Fair*), who, as Lord Yarmouth, was known by the Prince Regent as 'Red Herrings' or the 'Yarmouth Bloater'. It then became the Old Pulteney Hotel in which Czar Alexander of Russia stayed in 1814, after which it was, briefly, the British and Foreign Union Club in 1830.

The 4TH Marquess of Hertford got Thomas Cubitt to rebuild the house (on the same base and in similar bow-fronted style) in 1850–1, complete with a large picture gallery for the paintings that were to form the core of the Wallace Collection (whose founder, Sir Richard Wallace, the illegitimate son of the Marquess, inherited the house and the collection in 1872). The 4TH Marquess never lived here due to the unpleasant smell emitted by the Tyburn Stream (in fact a sewer, thankfully piped when the Underground was built) and the collection went to Manchester Square.

The house then passed to Julian Goldsmid MP, who had Alfred Waterhouse alter it and who lived there until his death in 1896. At that point the house became the *sportif* Isthmian Club and then, following further work (including the unfortunate addition of a rather soufflé-like mansard) in 1926-7, a hotel again – The Splendide, frequented by Cole Porter. In the 1970s and '80s, the house was occupied by the Arts Council. (The artist Joe Tilson recalls a huge boardroom table on the first floor, presided over by Sir William Coldstream flanked by artistic luminaries such as the aristocratic Sir John Pope-Hennessy and the youthful Nicholas Serota.) The building is now an elegant office building with some flats, taking a rest after all that history.

→ Pre-mansard halcyon days

↓ Mock Regency: James Gillray's caricature of Hellgate, Newgate and Cripplegate

↑ Grand hotel: the Czar's visit in 1814

↑ Swell Parties: American star Frances Day appearing at the Hotel Splendide, 1930s

33 Coventry House, 106 Piccadilly 1759–61

THIS IS one of my favourite buildings in Piccadilly, as much for its architecture as for its history and current use. The building stands on the site of the old Greyhound Inn and was built in 1759–61 for Sir Henry Hunlocke who sold it to the Earl of Coventry. He in turn commissioned Robert Adam to remodel the first-floor rooms (1765–70) (and much of his scheme survives). The Soane Museum has some wonderful Adam drawings for the house. Thomas Cundy made further alterations in 1810–11 and discreet wings were added at the back, but the height of the main building stayed the same – for once no Edwardian mansard soufflé! And Lady Coventry had an underground passage built below Piccadilly to the Deputy Ranger's Lodge in Green Park [*see also* **57**].

It was for many years the distinguished St. James's Club (so named because of its original location), which also housed the wonderful Dilettante Society portraits by George Knapton and Joshua Reynolds now hanging at Brooks's following the merger of the two clubs in 1975. The St. James's began as a diplomats' club (Comte Flahaut de la Billarderie, Napoléon III's ambassador to Britain, was a member) and then widened its membership base – which explains how Bolshevik Ivan Maisky and billionaire Nubar Gulbenkian were both members (as well as Lord Lucan, Ian Fleming, Evelyn Waugh, Osbert Lancaster and Osbert Sitwell). During World War II, the St. James's Club took in the Bachelors' Club [*see also* **44**]. The club had a French chef one of whose specialities was River Trout *Cléopâtre*, prepared with oysters. It was also the only club with a backgammon room.

In 2017, the building became the first school to open in Mayfair in two centuries – Eaton Square Upper School – educating 150 children in Grade 1 surroundings; hopefully the launchpad for generations of æsthetes. The extremely lucky headteacher has her study in Lady Coventry's gold-leaf and wood-panelled octagonal dressing room of 1765.

← Adam's ceiling with pictures by Antonio Zucchi

↓ Bags of talent: the new school

↑→ A Bolshevik and a billionaire: Maisky and Gulbenkian both belonged to the St. James's Club

34

Sheraton Grand Hotel 1925–7

THE PARK Lane Hotel (now known as the Sheraton Grand) (Henry Tanner, 1925–7) was the first hotel in London with a bathroom in every room. It filled a metal frame for a structure started in 1913–14, which had been abandoned when its German hotelier developer was interned as an 'enemy alien'. For 14 years the steel frame stood empty on Piccadilly, and was known as the 'Birdcage Hotel'.

It has a magnificent and dramatically subterranean Art Deco ballroom (Higgs & Hill, 1930–1) – the best Art Deco interior I have seen/danced in in England – all scallops, nymphs and wild beasts in silver, mauve and pink. During World War II it was designated to be the substitute venue for the House of Commons should Westminster be bombed. And the hotel has a number of other interesting and varied interiors – a veritable 1930s Disneyland – from the faux 17TH-century Oak Room to a 'Tudor Rose' French restaurant by Waring & Gillow and the Louis XV *boiseries* in the Grill Room, which had come from Pierpont Morgan's Kensington house. In the lane behind, there is a 1928 garage, with accommodation for Hispano Suizas and chauffeurs.

The hotel replaced several buildings (107–115 Piccadilly), the most important of which was № 107. This had, in 1814, been occupied by Field Marshall von Blücher on his visit to London for the festivities at the end of the Napoleonic Wars [*see also* **63**] and (while the Czar was staying at № 105) he would sit in an armchair at the top of the stairs smoking a pipe and greeting passers-by. It then became the home of Nathan Mayer Rothschild, the brilliant banker from Frankfurt who financed Waterloo and who once suggested to a self-important visitor that he should take two chairs. The 5TH Earl of Rosebery also lived here before becoming Prime Minister.

For a long time № 107 housed the Savile Club but it became structurally unsound while the hotel next door was being built and so the Savile moved to its current *dix-huitième* palace on Brook Street, allowing the hotel to expand into its slightly clumsy asymmetrical form.

The mansard, for once, is original. The cladding is ceramic stone. Numerous films have been shot here, including *The End of the Affair, Goldeneye, Brideshead Revisited* and *The Danish Girl*.

↓→ The Art Deco splendour of the ballroom

↓ The overmantel *boiserie* from J.P. Morgan's Kensington home

← An early view of the hotel before it was expanded. The Savile Club is still visible just to the right of the hotel

↓ The stretch of Piccadilly where the hotel now stands, c.1900. Coventry House **[33]** is on the far right

35 The Athenæum Hotel 1935–6

THE ATHENÆUM HOTEL is the latest of several Athenæa on this spot. The first was the Junior Athenæum Club (yet another 'entry level' club, this time for the glorious Athenæum on Waterloo Place). The club had bought Hope House (built 1848–49; French Renaissance; railings from Paris; faced in Caen Stone) on the death of MP Henry Thomas Hope, the son of the great designer Thomas Hope. The club retained on its façade the Hope crest: a bursting globe, and playful punning motto, '*At Spes infracta*' ('Yet my Hope is unbroken').

Hope House was lost and replaced in 1935–6 by a very moderne apartment building by Adie Button & Partners, Athenæum Court. In the 1970s and again in the 1990s, Athenæum Court was extensively modernised to become the Athenæum Hotel. The new hotel became a favourite among actors and directors, including De Niro, Spielberg, Brando, Bacall, Minnelli, Beatty, Kardashian and Taylor. According to the *Hollywood Reporter*, there were more film stars to be seen at the Athenæum than in the Polo Lounge at The Beverly Hills Hotel (another favourite of mine). In 2009, a living wall was installed outside the hotel, perhaps to evoke (in a vegetarian sort of way) distant memories of 'The Jungle', Rowland Ward's famed taxidermy emporium at 167 Piccadilly, a 100 years or so earlier.

The other distinguishing feature of the hotel is Jim, the 6ft 6in doorman, for 26 years the genial ginger-sideburned face of this end of Piccadilly, who is often to be seen standing next to the original penny-farthing bicycle on the pavement outside.

← Hope House, early 20TH century

← Naturally Piccadilly: the living wall

↓ Athenæum Court in the 1930s

← Piccadilly Jim

36 117-118 Piccadilly *1872*

THIS END of Piccadilly (from Down Street to Apsley House) – once a rather scrappy mix of coaching inns and tenements – became increasingly grand in the 19TH century and was known as Piccadilly Terrace.

117–118 Piccadilly is by C.A. Buckler, 1872, 'in a grave old-fashioned Italianizing style' (Pevsner). It is rather extraordinary that this formal elegance is a mere 10 years before the full-on neo-Elizabethan bling of 100 Piccadilly [30]. № 117 was once occupied by Lord O'Neill, Prebendary of Christ Church, Dublin, and an authority on ecclesiastical music; and then by Hugh Childers, who had various posts (including Home Secretary and Chancellor of the Exchequer) under William Gladstone. The building was also the United Empire Club at one point [*see* 31] and later housed the National Society of Day Nurseries.

Its most interesting moment was when, briefly, from 1919–20, it became the about-to-be, and then the newly established League of Nations (the precursor to the United Nations) before its move to Geneva.

№ 118 now houses the delicious Peruvian restaurant, Coya.

Round the corner in Down Street is the disused Down Street tube station, at one point Churchill's bunker during World War II.

→ The library of the League of Nations, 1920

↑ Downing Street to Down Street: signage from 1939 when the station was converted for wartime use

← The disused Down Street Underground station can be seen at the lower right

37

119 Piccadilly *1870s*

119 PICCADILLY CONTINUES the parade of sober (and rather dull) Italianate buildings. Even though it has quite different detailing on the façade when compared with Nos 117–118, a clever device has, more recently, been added to sew the terrace together at street level: Nos 118 and 119 share an Ionic portico, even though their façades above are quite different.

This is a building with a true heritage of modern transportation. Between 1902 and 1908, it was the (from 1907, Royal) Automobile Club, a club that became so popular that it soon had to move to its own new palatial building on Pall Mall, designed by the same architects as The Ritz [17] but even larger, where it still resides today.

After a few years as the Cavendish Club, the building became the Royal Aero Club, a club founded in 1902 and whose members included many of the fathers of mechanised aviation in Britain – Charles Rolls (as in Royce, and famously mean, bringing his own sandwiches to the club and ordering a glass of water before leaving without having spent anything – which led the club to introduce a cover charge), the Short brothers, Frederick Handley Page and Baron Brabazon. The club was regulator (issuing pilot licences), promoter (sponsoring a competition to design the first aircraft seatbelt and epic trips to New Zealand, Australia and South Africa) as well as gentleman's club. It also effectively organised much of the recruitment for the country's first air force during World War I. Eventually, in 1961, it merged with the Lansdowne Club, which for several years retained many of its artefacts – such as Louis Blériot's propeller, which still hangs in the bar.

→ Turning its back on horse-drawn locomotion: the Automobile Club, c.1905

↑ Different façades but a shared portico with № 118

↑ Racing Down Under in 1953

38 The Cavalry and Guards Club 1888

AFTER ALL that motorised locomotion next door, we return to equine and pedestrian traditions at The Cavalry and Guards Club. (Lejeune noted the 'high degree of hippophilia' among its members, even though the regiments had long since been mechanised.) This is the last functioning great Victorian club on Piccadilly, huge and bustling. And during Lockdown, when every other club was closed, it was putting up military personnel so that they could be close to their work – and, with great style and pride, the porters were still wearing their tail coats and keeping the flag flying outside.

Not being in the least military, I am fascinated by this club and have thoroughly enjoyed the times I have spent here. It has a truly magnificent long dining room overlooking Green Park. But it is the militaria that set this club apart. They start with the cannon ball name plates (*see illustration p.162*) in the portico outside and then it is battle after battle and charge after charge on canvas, distinguished soldiers in bronze, a stirring sculpture of a Cavalry charger with an empty saddle (a memorial to fallen members) and another, *The Last Call,* of a trumpeter dying as his horse collapses under him (*see opposite*). In *I May Be Some Time,* Titus Oates is shown manfully getting lost in a blizzard. There is one room – the Field Marshal's Room – entirely lined with portraits of cavalry field marshals.

The experience of going there reminds me of driving in the official car lanes during the Olympic Games. Using those reserved lanes in 2012 made one feel healthy and athletic – luncheon at the Cavalry and Guards Club makes one feel faintly heroic and historic ... or at least stand with one's shoulders straightened. It is a welcome relief after the heartburn induced by the average club lunch elsewhere.

The first known inhabitant of this site (c. 1715), was a watchmaker, Abraham Isaacs. By the end of the 18TH century, an auctioneer named James Daniels lived here. So skilled was he that he was described as being able to 'pick one's pocket with his tongue'. Between 1823 and 1875 the building was a lodging house.

The club was built in 1888 by Adolphus Croft of Gillow & Co. briefly as a mansion and then as the club. It started with only five bays and then was doubled in 1908 to 9 + 1 bays by Mewès & Davis (the American architects of The Ritz [17] and the Royal Automobile Club in Pall Mall) who also added the elegant Georgian style interiors. The Cavalry Club and the Guards Club merged in 1976.

39 The Royal Air Force Club 1888

PER ARDUA AD ASTRA proclaims the façade of the RAF Club, which in 2018 turned 100. Artistically, this is an airborne version of its neighbour, the Cavalry and Guards Club [38], a shrine to military flight – from Frank Wootton's triptych of the Battle of Britain, to contemporary stained-glass windows by Helen Whittaker aglow with Harriers, propellers and dials, *sotto in su* Bristol Fighters circling the chandeliers in the ballroom and a treasury of silver aeroplanes in the bar.

The hallways of this shrine are lined with hundreds of squadron badges with mottos such as *Semper Aggressus* and *Nihil Nos Effugit*. My favourite badge is that of Squadron 460 of the Royal Australian Air Force: a kangaroo salient above a boomerang with the motto "Strike and Return".

The building itself was constructed as two townhouses by Adolphus Croft of Gillow & Co. in 1888 on the site of an old tavern, The Running Horse (the name of which is kept alive in that of the basement pub of the club, where 18TH-century pewter tankards from the original tavern discovered during excavations in the 1920s are displayed). From 1784 to 1851, № 124 was the premises of the remarkable manufacturer of locks, water closets and the gates of the Wellington Arch [54] and Marble Arch [49], founded by Joseph Bramah. The two houses were merged in 1892 to form club premises: first (and briefly) the Piccadilly Club, followed by the Imperial Services Club and then the Ladies' Lyceum Club. In 1919–22 the building was remodelled by Sir Aston Webb (architect of the main façade of Buckingham Palace and of Admiralty Arch) for the RAF Club, introducing a simplified 18TH-century æsthetic. And, in 1968, John Winter (who had worked for Charles Eames, Skidmore, Owings & Merrill and Ernö Goldfinger) carried out what looks like a very refined modernisation in which classical features were retained alongside modern furniture.

The building also has a very pretty second entrance in Old Park Lane which used to be the ladies' door.

←↑ John Winter's elegant 1968 interiors

→ The former ladies' entrance in Old Park Lane

40

1 Old Park Lane 1914

FROM RAF TO ROCK, this is the first of the two Hard Rock premises that so enticingly frame the entrance to what used to be the beginning of Park Lane – modern aristocracy effortlessly taking over from old-world aristocracy.

1 Old Park Lane was built in 1914 and designed by Delissa Joseph. Palmer & Holden reworked the ground floor for Coutts & Co. Bank in 1923. In 2003 the building became apartments, with the USP of having Hard Rock retail amenities below.

Coutts's night safe-deposit box remains in the wall outside and a visit into the shop is as rewarding for the rock 'n' roll *aficionado* as it is for the architectural-historical *flâneur:* portraits of musical legends cavort among the classical mouldings of the banking hall, while in the vaults below, strongboxes that once glistened with Mayfair's crystals now display relics of the Sex Pistols.

The previous house had been built in 1793 and was first occupied by Sir John Lade, a member of the 'ultra-fast set surrounding the Prince Regent' (Dasent). Samuel Johnson had a low opinion of Sir John's intellect and when asked by him whether he should marry, advised that he 'would advise no man to marry who is not likely to propagate understanding'. Johnson also wrote the poem *One and Twenty* about the coming of age of this profligate. An inveterate gambler and a skilled horse breeder and driver, Sir John would dress in riding clothes at all times, carrying a whip wherever he went. He scandalously married the beautiful Lætitia Derby, who had been the mistress of highwayman 'Sixteen String Jack' Rann as well as of the Duke of York. She was a great favourite of the Prince Regent (who commissioned George Stubbs to paint her portrait) and was also an excellent horse driver. The violence of her language was such that it gave rise to the expression 'to swear like Letty Lade'. Having gambled away his money, Sir John spent some time in a debtors' jail and was awarded a pension by the Prince Regent as his 'driving tutor' under the name The Reverend Doctor Tolly.

After Sir John, the house was inhabited by the Margrave of Ansbach who was also ruler of Bayreuth, a surprising musical lineage for this temple to rock 'n' roll.

➔ 'Pomp and pleasure, pride and plenty'; Sir John Lade by Joshua Reynolds

➔ From profligacy to economy: Coutts & Co. in the 1960s with a handsome Mercedes W109 parked outside

➔ Lætitia Lade by George Stubbs

➔ Safe keeping: Sex Pistols relics under lock and key

41 The Hard Rock Café 1905

IN TIMES of Lockdown one was constantly reminded of all the things in life one had not experienced: Angkor Wat, the Great Wall of China, Vladivostok... and as I wrote about this building, I was hit by the realisation that I had never dined at the Hard Rock Café. And this Hard Rock Café is not any old Hard Rock Café – it is the original one, founded in 1971, the Jerusalem of the hamburger and a place filled with as many relics as The Vatican. And, since 2007, when it was acquired by the Seminole Tribe of Florida, it has become the *de facto* Native American embassy in Mayfair – perfect symmetry given that much of Florida once belonged to the Duke of Westminster.

And the building! If there was ever a piece of Edwardian post modernism, then this has to be it – that soaring exuberance, that orgy of decoration, those stripes, and also that zany discipline! Pevsner describes it as a 'remarkable freak'. Edward VII loathed how it had ruined his view across the gardens at Buckingham Palace.

The current building was designed by Collcutt & Hamp in 1905, originally with a car showroom downstairs and (as is still the case) apartments upstairs. (Collcut & Hamp also designed the 'savagely ungraceful' New Adelphi off the Strand [Pevsner] and the river front of The Savoy.) It replaced the 18TH-century Gloucester House, which had been rented by Lord Elgin in 1806. In the garden, Lord Elgin had a shed built to display the Parthenon Marbles, just arrived in Britain. The precursor of the modern 'blockbuster' show, this display (1807–1816) proved to be hugely popular. So much so that, in June 1808, a famous prize fighter posed naked in front of the marbles enabling a select audience to compare the carving of the antiquities to his finely honed body. Byron however was fiercely critical of the whole enterprise, referring to the display as 'a general mart, for all the mutilated blocks of art'.

The house was occupied by Prince William, Duke of Gloucester and Edinburgh, from 1816–34 and then by Prince George, Duke of Cambridge, until his death in 1904.

I resolved, when the Lockdown finished, to visit the café and to order 'One Night in Bangkok' followed by a 'Local Legendary' while thinking of Lord Elgin's original hard rocks.

↓ Proto-PoMo: Collcut & Hamp's remarkable pediment

→ The stuff of dreams

↑ Entrance to the apartments

↑ Chiselled features, 400BC

← Chiselled features, AD1905

42 138 Piccadilly *1757, 1888*

138 PICCADILLY WAS once (with № 139 next door) the house of the 'wicked Old Q', the 'Star of Piccadilly', the 4TH Duke of Queensberry (1724–1810), voluptuary *extraordinaire* and for 28 years Lord of the Bedchamber to George III. Old Q would sit at his first-floor bow window (or at his balcony with a parasol, weather permitting) on the lookout for beautiful women as they passed below, every now and then dispatching his liveried running footman after one of them (Old Q was said to be the last man in London to keep running footmen) with a hastily penned *billet-doux*. He had an outside staircase fitted from the first floor down to Piccadilly to facilitate his amorous endeavours.

Old Q was also addicted to wagers, on one occasion betting a friend that he could make a letter travel 50 miles in an hour and winning the bet by enclosing the letter in a cricket ball and engaging 20 cricketers to throw the ball among themselves, at speed and with great accuracy, for an hour. On another occasion his neighbour Sir John Lade [*see* **40**] bet him 1,000 Guineas that he could not find a man who could eat more in a meal sitting. Once again Old Q won 'by a pig and an apple pie'.

Old Q's house was built in 1757 by Matthew Brettingham (the architect of Holkham Hall). Its brick façade was refaced in stone in 1888 by R.S. Wornum with the current giant Doric pilasters and the cornicing that ties it to № 139 next door [**43**], now a separate building. In a possible act of revenge, the ladies' Lyceum Club took over the building in the 1920s. The Dracula Society (and many other vampirical authorities) claim that this is Count Dracula's house in Bram Stoker's novel, the fictional '347 Piccadilly'.

The building is now occupied by EON Productions, formed by the late Cubby Broccoli, Michael Wilson (also a preeminent 19TH-century photography collector) and Barbara Broccoli, and which produces and owns the copyright to James Bond Films, taking us straight from Old Q to new Q.

→ *A Worn-out Debauchée,* Thomas Rowlandson's caricature of Old Q, c.1790

43

139 Piccadilly 1757, 1888

139 PICCADILLY (formerly 13 Piccadilly Terrace) was the other half of Old Q's house [42] but was separated shortly after he died. From 1815, it became Lord Byron's house (Byron having moved up the street from A.2 Albany) and there he wrote *Parisina* and *The Siege of Corinth*, published by Byron's friend John Murray of 50 Albermarle Street. While living here, he had a daughter (Ada Lovelace – who was to become a celebrated mathematician and pioneer of computing), met Walter Scott, separated from his wife and was served with 16 writs. He then left England never to return.

After Byron's departure it became the 4TH Earl of Rosebery's house and, around 1890, the house of Sir Algernon Borthwick, the proprietor of the *Morning Post*, a further link in the tradition of newspaper proprietors living on Green Park.

'La Fiamma' (The Flame – on account of her hair colour), Baroness d'Erlanger, took the house around 1900, her other house being Andrea Palladio's Villa Malcontenta. Here she established a famous salon and supported artists including Cecil Beaton, Philip de László and Sergei Diaghilev. Later in life the Baroness moved to Hollywood where she established the first gay bar in Los Angeles, the Café Gala. Her daughter Baba was part of Beaton's circle of bright young things and was photographed by him and painted by Augustus John, and later became a patron of Salvador Dalí and Man Ray.

The current façade is from 1888 and rather neatly ties this house to its erstwhile other half by sharing a cornice, but also asserts its independence with its Ionic pilasters in contrast to the Doric ones next door.

↑ Lord Byron

↓ Caricature in *Vanity Fair* of Algernon Borthwick, 1871

↑ 'La Fiamma' By William Bruce Ellis Ranken, 1918

→ Baba, Baroness d'Erlanger, 1922

← Ada Lovelace, c.1850

44 140 Piccadilly 1874–6

140 PICCADILLY WRAPS around the corner of Hamilton Place. Its rather French elegance prepares one for the glamour of Hamilton Place and the magnificent former Rothschild mansions (those that have survived are now Les Ambassadeurs and The Royal Aeronautical Society, although most of the street is now occupied by the InterContinental [45] and The Four Seasons hotels). № 140 is now the office of the Olayan Group, a family-owned multinational Saudi conglomerate.

The first house on this spot was built in the mid-18TH century and accommodated an assortment of Cavendishes and Dukes (Dorset/Gordon), MPs (John Ramsden and Edward Kerrison) and other notables. The house shrank when Hamilton Place was widened in the 19TH century (it used to be the main route to Park Lane).

The current incarnation of the house dates from 1874–6 (architect: R.M. Marsh) and a few years later became the Bachelors' Club, which required members who decided to marry to pay a fine in order to be allowed to remain in the club [*see also* 33]. At some point in World War II, it merged with the St. James's Club at 106 Piccadilly [*see* 33], after the building had been 'requisitioned' (though it is not clear for what purpose).

№ 140 then assumes mysterious associations. In 1942 it appears on the cover of pro-French liberation pamphlet — the *Song of the Free French* — by Aleister Crowley (*'Créateur du Signe V'* — I assume Victory rather than the other V sign). Crowley was also a founder of the 'Thelema' religion and a magician, occultist, mountaineer, painter, novelist and spy (which is perhaps why he was issuing this pamphlet from a requisitioned building).

Things became even more mysterious in the 1970s, when № 140 became the world headquarters of the Planet of the Apes Fan Club – it is unclear whether this club adopted the format of a classic Piccadilly gentleman's/apes' club (leather armchairs, claret and bunches of bananas) or perhaps sought to recreate a more tropical feel (think Trader Vic's up the street).

← Francophilia on Piccadilly.

↓ Members only

↑ The mysterious Aleister Crowley and his pro-liberation pamphlet.

45

InterContinental London Park Lane 1968–75

BUILDING A 440-room hotel on this stretch of Piccadilly is like cooking a risotto – it must absorb gallons of intensely flavoured history; in this case, four large town houses on a prime piece of Piccadilly and several on Hamilton Place. The resulting 1968–75 dish by Sir Frederick Gibberd (a little forgotten now but very successful as the architect of Liverpool Metropolitan Cathedral, The London Central Mosque, Heathrow Airport and Harlow New Town), while elegant and timeless, does not quite have the depth of flavour one would hope for. But it does have quite a pleasingly textured façade and its stepped bays evoke the terrace of townhouses that preceded it. So, in terms of the buildings it replaced, here goes:

142 Piccadilly: Alice de Rothschild's house, which she bought in 1866 after the death of her sister-in-law, Evelina, to be closer to her widowed brother Ferdinand de Rothschild.

143 Piccadilly: Ferdinand de Rothschild bought this house in 1865 and filled it with wonderful French furniture, much of which went to his country house, Waddesdon Manor [*see* **11**], where it can still be seen today. The house was by George Dance. A piece of its railing survives in the Soane Museum.

144 Piccadilly: 'Hippiedilly'! Built in the 1790s by Sir Drummond Smith, it was Lord Palmerston's house during the Crimean War before he moved up the street to Cambridge House [27]. Bombed during The War, it became the Arts Educational School where Jane Seymour and Nigel Havers trained. In 1969 it became a colossal hippie squatter camp, flying the Hell's Angels flag, under Sid Rawle, who wanted, '144 [Piccadilly] to become a permanent urban guerrilla base for underground activities'. The squat had a drawbridge for access by its population of 100, while *The People* frowned: 'Drug taking, couples making love while others look on, a heavy mob armed with iron bars, filth and stench, foul language'. The squat was eventually dispersed by the police and redeveloped by Eric Lyons.

145 Piccadilly: Princesses Elizabeth (now Queen Elizabeth II) and Margaret's childhood home before World War II until, unexpectedly, their father became King following the abdication of Edward VIII in 1936.

↑ Hippiedilly, 1969

↓ The future: King George VI leaves № 145 to attend the Accession Council, December 1936, following the abdication of King Edward VIII

→↓ Ferdinand de Rothschild, banker, art collector and politician. The terrace, shortly before demolition in the 1960s

46 The Gap 1961

THIS ENTRY is about a gap in what, until 1961, was part of Piccadilly and overlooked Green Park.

During the late 19TH century/early 20TH century this was known as Rothschild Row [*see also* **44**]. At № 148 lived Lionel de Rothschild. He had bought the house in 1840 and expanded it by the addition of № 147 in 1859–60 following the death of its occupant, Vice-Admiral John Tollemache. The house, refurbished by Thomas Cubitt, was lavishly decorated in French style and had a butler named Toogood.

Next door at № 146 was Sir Edmond Antrobus MP, whose father had made his fortune in sugar plantations in the West Indies (and on emancipation had received compensation for losing 500 slaves). In addition to 146 Piccadilly, Sir Edmond owned Stonehenge and at one point is said to have almost sold the stones to an American collector.

Earlier in the 19TH century, № 147 had been the property of Charles Alexandre de Calonne, Louis XVI's Prime Minister and Comptroller of Finances, who had fled France in 1787 and for whom Sir John Soane designed a chimney piece. Soane had also worked on Nos 146 and 148 and John Adam had designed a screen for the street elevation of № 147.

Several properties in the row were damaged during World War II. In 1958, London County Council announced that it would demolish Nos 146–48 in order to improve the traffic flow from Hyde Park Corner to Marble Arch, thereby stranding Apsley House and also slicing off a piece of Hyde Park in order to accommodate the new northbound lanes of Park Lane. Hyde Park's previous boundary lay in what is now the central reservation of Park Lane.

One weekend during the Lockdown, in a return to ancient times, I followed a green woodpecker up the central reservation of the suddenly deserted Park Lane.

Perhaps, I mused, if this Lockdown continues and traffic becomes a thing of the past, we could fill this gap with some magnificent contemporary town houses.

→ End of terrace: Apsley House, near left, c.1910

↓ John Adam's design for a screen for № 147

↑ London County Council perpetuated the trend of destruction pioneered in World War II

← Piccadilly, c.1930, before the gap and the underpass, and with the Wellington Arch **[54]** still in Green Park

Apsley House 1826–30

UNTIL 1771, this plot contained the Hyde Park Lodge, a collapsing apple stall and the Hercules' Pillars Inn. The freehold for the apple stall had been given by George II to an old soldier he had recognised as having served at Dettingen. In front was the Piccadilly Turnpike marking the entrance to London. Being on higher land, the house had 'fine views over the Surrey and Kent hills' (Shepard).

The first house was built in brick in 1771–8 for Lord Apsley (then Chancellor) by the Adam brothers and was only five bays wide (see Meissen plate, right). The house was bought in 1807 by Marquess Wellesley, the Duke of Wellington's brother and overhauled by James Wyatt. The Duke bought the house from his brother after the wars and commissioned Benjamin Dean and James Wyatt to enlarge it to its current seven-bay Palladian style, facing it with Bath stone (1826–30). (The Wyatts also worked on Lancaster House [1].) Daily, the Duke would ride out into the park in a blue frock coat, white waistcoat and trousers.

The house has only ever been inhabited by two families. Although now the Wellington Museum, the Wellesleys live on the second floor and use the garden.

The museum is one of my favourites – wonderful paintings, china, silver and Napoleonica including a group of Spanish masters rescued from Napoléon by Wellington at Vitoria and given to him by the King of Spain and a Titian, Romano etc., etc. The staircase is dominated by a colossal (3.45m tall) marble statue of *Napoléon as Mars the Peacemaker* by Canova – how curious (not to say kinky) to have a giant effigy of one's life enemy standing naked in one's hall.

Apsley House changed appearance in the early 1960s when it was cut off from Piccadilly [see 46]. Visually, it went from end of terrace to freestanding country house and so an east façade had to be created (with blind windows) and, at the front, handsome Egyptian-style railings installed to match those of the park gates. While quite isolated, it is no longer dominated by its taller neighbour and sits well alongside the equally classical Lanesborough Hotel.

• • •

This brings us to the end of Piccadilly and this side of Green Park.

↓ Piccadilly pre-1771: the apple stall

← The side façade added in the 1960s when Apsley House became free-standing

↓ Emperor's New Clothes: *Napoléon as Mars the Peacemaker* by Canova dominates the staircase

↑ The loveliest garden in London

48 Buckingham Palace 1825–30

THERE IS only one building overlooking the third (and final) side of Green Park and that is Buckingham Palace.

I will not attempt to write a history of the Palace in a single chapter but will instead ask you to focus on the part of the Palace most visible from the park (the main façade looks down the Mall). Mercifully, the park side is much prettier than Sir Aston Webb's rather thumping and proto-Ceaușescu-esque front of 1913. 'Our' side is in fact part of John Nash's 1825–1830 scheme for George IV. From the park you can clearly see how that scheme, in its warm Bath stone with all its delicate detailing and its human scale, collides with the cold Edwardian Portland stone bling of the front (which was added to another unsuccessful façade (by Edward Blore) over only 13 weeks in the Summer of 1913). The stylistic collision is as dramatic when seen from the air. It is a daily relief to us Green Parkites that the Bucharestification never went any further.

The screen, topped by the lion and the unicorn, with its (surprisingly) cast-iron Doric columns below, serves as the entrance to the garden of Buckingham Palace, in which the true elegance of Nash's scheme can be seen in a magical park-like setting.

• • •

This chapter brings me to the end of our 48-course menu round Green Park. But, as with all copious meals, I think we deserve a few petits fours *to help us stumble home and so, as a second part to this account, I will show you some monuments and other structures in and around Green Park.*

→ Nash's screen

↑→ Shock of the new: Webb's facade collides with Nash's earlier work, which still forms the majority of the Palace

A view across Green Park towards Westminster Cathedral, c.1925, with the beginnings of The Pantheon **[64]** in the foreground

[PART II]

Monuments and Structures of Green Park

49 Marble Arch 1827–30

IN THE late 1830s and 1840s, one of the most visible monuments from the Buckingham Palace [48] side of Green Park would have been what we now call Marble Arch. Before the courtyard of Buckingham Palace was enclosed by the block that supports the current façade, this triumphal arch stood at its entrance. It only spent 17 years there, and has now spent 170 years in the rather less hospitable environment at the top of Park Lane, stranded 'twixt Hyde Park and Primark.

The story of the arch is one of unfulfilled ambition and compromise. George IV commissioned John Nash to design the arch as part of the grandiose reworking of Buckingham Palace. The model in the V&A shows an altogether more elaborate and decorated affair: John Flaxman devised an intricate decorative scheme to cover the surfaces of the arch commemorating key victories in the Napoleonic Wars (Trafalgar/Nelson/naval themes *recto;* Waterloo/Wellington/army *verso*).

And yet even as built (after King George died and Nash was fired) it is quite grand: it is the first building in England to be clad entirely in white Carrara and each column is made of a single block of marble. The gates are by Bramah & Sons, whose premises were on Piccadilly [*see* 39] and who produced the gates for the Wellington Arch [54] and for Decimus Burton's screen next to Apsley House.

Though all were carved, only a few sculptures from the original design were installed on the arch – partly because the disgruntled Nash would not explain where they all fitted. And so they were given away and repurposed. George was made to sit on his horse in a corner of Trafalgar Square and the (then new) National Gallery incorporated in its façade a number of winged victories pacified for their new location (in one case having been retrofitted with an easel and brushes – make art, not war). Britannia had her trident removed and was given a spear to become Minerva, goddess of Wisdom. Another frieze became a flower planter at an office development on the Euston Road – Regency flower power.

The Arch was moved in 1850 by Nash's pupil, Thomas Cubitt, to become an entrance to the Great Exhibition. It is now an endearing structure, refusing to give up despite its miserable surroundings, no doubt dreaming of those happy years spent on the edge of Green Park.

→ The arch in its original place at the entrance to Buckingham Palace **[48]**

↑ The V&A model with statuary and reliefs in their intended positions

↑ Lucky escape: George IV outside St-Martin-in-the-Fields

→ Wise Britannia: Minerva atop the National Gallery

50 Canada Gate 1905–11

THE GRAND central avenue of Green Park, the Broad Walk, which links Piccadilly and Buckingham Palace, was planted in 1905. While the Piccadilly end is marked by the elegant 18TH-century Devonshire Gates [25], the Canada Gate at Buckingham Palace is an essay in Edwardian flamboyance.

The gates belong to Sir Aston Webb's Victoria Memorial scheme, the mighty Carrara monument to the Queen-Empress and to all things colonial, complete with its 'bosomy ships' prows' (Pevsner).

The gates were presented to London by Canada, at the time the senior Dominion of the British Empire. They were designed by Alfred Drury, who also did the West Africa and South Africa Gates on the other side of the memorial (the last, Australia, is by Derwent Wood) and numerous other Edwardian heroic sculptures around Whitehall and Piccadilly.

These are the most splendid of the various gates in the scheme and prepare the Green Park stroller for (or perhaps protect him or her from) all the colossal magnificence on the other side. Two not-very-Canadian-looking Portland stone cherubim (one with fruit, the other with a fishing net and a seal) sit at either end of the line-up of the emblems of the seven Canadian provinces of the time.

I particularly like the gilt bison (emblem of Manitoba), which looks as if it has been dragged all the way from the prairies to Harrods for a full Al-Fayed makeover. Endearingly and enduringly preposterous!

↑ A fruity cherub stands guard

↗ Edward VII's cypher

→ Manitoba bling

51 Canada Memorial 1994

JUST BEHIND the Canada Gate [50] is the Canada Memorial. We move from the Imperial 'one size (subject to the odd seal or kangaroo) fits all' approach of the gates to a much more personal, intimate and one-off monument.

The work of Pierre Granche (1948–1997), a Québécois sculptor (there are wonderful works of his in Montréal, including in the metro), the memorial commemorates the 1 million Canadians who fought on the Allied side in the two world wars and the 113,000 who died. It rises from the park like the prow of a ship, with a ceremonial path orientated towards Halifax in Nova Scotia, the embarkation point of most of the soldiers. It is made of red Canadian granite and accommodates a fountain that washes over inset maple leaves of bronze; the materials come from Canada and were shipped from Halifax.

In a city of neo-classical monuments, this is a rare example of a modern abstract piece (although there have been a couple of powerful examples more recently: the New Zealand Memorial on Hyde Park Corner and the 7 July Memorial in Hyde Park). It is also a piece that fits into the park without taking over – it appears to be half buried and its shiny surfaces reflect and integrate their surroundings – and that engages with the viewer. Children are fascinated by being able to walk through the planes of flowing water at eye level.

All of this is in such delightful contrast to some of the immense and pompous memorials that have been dumped elsewhere in our parks.

↓ The ceremonial path is orientated towards Halifax, Nova Scotia

↑ Canadian corner: the Canada Gate **[50]** lies just beyond the Canada Memorial

→ Inset bronze maple leaf

52 Tea Kiosks 2018–19

THE TEA KIOSK near the Canada Gate (one of a pair – 2018 and 2019) is the latest structure in Green Park.

It works rather well. Warm, soft and organic, its shape echoes those of the surrounding trees and their canopies. It is made of multiple layers of bentwood, which makes it both dense and light, like the branches of the trees around it.

There is also something inherently cosy and appropriate about a wooden structure, especially when it sits in London's most elegantly understated park. It is the antithesis of the insensitive and bombastic Bomber Command Memorial at the other end of the park [SS].

Wooden tea kiosks are very much a part of the streetscape of London – how we love taxi drivers' kiosks – and that also makes these structures immediately appealing. And of course the bentwood construction evokes the classic Thonet café chair and makes one want to sit down with a cup of tea or coffee.

The kiosks were designed by the Anglo-Maltese Mizzi Studio and built by Tom Raffield of Cornwall, a company that specialises in bentwood furniture and lighting. Variants have been installed in St. James's Park and Hyde Park.

↑ The Thonet *No. 14 chair*, 1859

Traditional taxi drivers' kiosk

53 Commonwealth Memorial Gate 2001–2

THE EARLY 2000s saw a building boom of mostly hideous and outsized monuments to every possible aspect of World War II (reaching its most absurd level in the Animals in War Memorial in Park Lane with its weird inscription: 'They had no choice' – implying that the human victims of war had blithely volunteered their lives). Acres of London parkland were covered in stone, sacrificing local amenity in order to humour random pressure groups from goodness knows where. It all felt like a rather pathetic way of Britain trying to evoke its one time military might and position as a superpower just as the tragedy of the Iraq war was starting – the yang to the yin of Cool Britannia.

Some of these memorials, thankfully, are beautiful. Most of them, sadly, are populist *Schmalz*.

The Commonwealth Memorial Gate at the top of Constitution Hill, which celebrates the Empire Forces of World War II, is at the better end of the spectrum. First, because, as a gateway, it has a purpose as a marker of the car and bicycle entrance into the processional area around Green Park and the Palace (and shuts out the traffic at weekends) – bringing visual definition and interest to the otherwise rather dreary and endless wall around the Palace gardens. Also, because it does not intrude on the smallest Royal park in London (Green Park is approximately ⅛TH the size of Hyde Park). And, most importantly, because it is probably the most elegant and well executed of the various neo-classical memorials of this period.

It was designed by Liam O'Connor and built in 2001–2. It has the paired-down classical look and feel of Edwin Lutyens and Herbert Baker – especially in the four urn-topped columns honouring the 5 million fighters from the Indian subcontinent, Africa and the Caribbean who served in the war (although, disappointingly, the neo-Mughal *chhattri*, by the side, is æsthetically rather puny by comparison).

When next you drive, or are driven, through these gates into the enclosure around Green Park and the Palace, reflect on the fact that it was only in 1889 that this roadway was opened to general use. Before that, only those who had been issued with ivory tickets by the Monarch were allowed to do so.

↓ The columns carry the names of Commonwealth nations that supported the war effort

↑ The dome of the *chhattri* is lined with the names of distinguished Commonwealth soldiers

↓ Grace and favour: a ticket to use Constitution Hill

54 Wellington Arch 1826–29

THE WELLINGTON ARCH (Decimus Burton, 1826–29) was for many years the entrance to Green Park having originally been intended as an entrance to the Palace and aligned with Burton's screen next to Apsley House. It was moved to its current position at the top of Constitution Hill in 1883.

The wonderful gates (also designed by Burton) were built by Bramah & Sons. This extraordinary business, established in 1784 at 124 Piccadilly and which still exists in Fitzrovia, also made the gates for Marble Arch [49], the railings for Burton's screen opposite and bullet-proof shutters for Apsley House [47]. From 1801, the company displayed in its window in Piccadilly a lock promising 200 Guineas to anyone able to pick it – a challenge taken up in 1851 by American locksmith Alfred Charles Hobbs, who managed to pick the lock after 51 hours' work over 16 days, while visiting London for the Great Exhibition.

In 1912 the arch was topped by Adrian Jones's *Peace Descending on the Quadriga of War*, apparently the largest bronze statue in Europe. Burton had intended a smaller one, which was never installed as the money for it (and other decorations) was withheld by the Treasury due to cost overruns here and at the Palace. Instead, a huge equestrian statue of Wellington by Matthew Cotes Wyatt was (to Burton's consternation) placed on the archway in 1845, where it remained until the arch was moved in 1883. It was so large that when it was still in the artist's studio, 12 men dined inside the horse (only three could take tea in the mould for one of Jones's horses). The statue was much derided on account of its size but, when Queen Victoria proposed to remove it, the Duke of Wellington declared that he would resign all his public posts if this happened and so Her Majesty backed down.

The arch was cut off from Green Park in 1961 to sit on its current island. Unlike Marble Arch, however, this island is constantly used by pedestrians, cyclists and riders as a means of getting from Hyde Park to Green Park and so the arch is used as much as ever.

Once a police station, it is now a delightful little museum and viewing platform, with the north side of the arch having been gutted and turned into a vent for the 1962 Piccadilly underpass.

↓ Decimus Burton's original design shows a smaller quadriga and more decorated surfaces

→ Big News: Wyatt's statue depicted in the *Illustrated London News*, 1846

THE ILLUSTRATED LONDON NEWS

No. 231.—Vol. IX.] FOR THE WEEK ENDING SATURDAY, OCTOBER 3, 1846. [SIXPENCE.

← The arch marking the entrance to Green Park before the installation of Adrian Jones's statue in 1912

↑ M.C. Wyatt's outsized statue of Wellington with Apsley House in view

55 Bomber Command Memorial 2011

Everything about the Bomber Command Memorial is hideous. It is an immense 85 metres long – too large to photograph straight on. Its detailing and architectural language are terrible (dainty faux Victorian lamps sitting on heavy bunches of classical columns and a colonnade stuck on to the main pavilion almost by accident). Its positioning, overlooking the Piccadilly underpass from the side, is random and without purpose. The sculpture inside is a hybrid of tabloid heroic (Our Boys...) and spooky Soviet realism. And the fact that it was built as recently as 2011 (by Liam O'Connor of the Commonwealth Memorial Gate, [53]) is profoundly depressing.

This monument came about as a result of a campaign mounted by *The Daily Telegraph* and *Daily Express*, veterans and others; it was strongly opposed by residents as well as heritage and garden conservation societies. That Westminster Council allowed it (and that the then Mayor of London was too weak to make any pronouncement on it) is indicative of our authorities' profound architectural ignorance and bad taste, which is resulting in so much of Central London becoming uglier and uglier (look at the æsthetically second-rate redevelopment of the area around Victoria Station).

Bomber Command is a difficult cause to celebrate. It is clearly tragic that 55,000 airmen died. Much of their work was essential in determining the outcome of the war. And yet, the systematic bombing of Dresden, Lübeck and other beautiful places is one of the great cultural and humanitarian disasters of the 20TH century.

If one just focuses on the airmen who gave their lives, how sad it is that their memory is kept alive by a structure so mediocre, in a place halfway between the beautiful and thoughtful Canada Memorial [51] and Decimus Burton's exquisitely graceful (and far smaller) screen on Hyde Park Corner.

How disappointing that a large piece of Green Park has been destroyed for this display of vulgarity (numerous mature trees had to be removed) and how insensitively the pompous mass of this edifice clashes with the bucolic informality of the park.

→ This glimpse of sky provides a moment of relief to the visitor

↑ The colonnade's collision with the main pavillion

↑ The curious combination of faux Victorian lanterns and clustered classical columns

56

Porters' Rest 1861

On Piccadilly on the edge of Green Park just opposite the Cavalry and Guards Club, stands this porters' rest. An inscription says that it was erected in 1861 by the Vestry of St. George's, Hanover Square *'for the benefit of porters and others carrying burdens'*.

I have long been fascinated by the licenced meat porters (known as 'bummarees' and whose act of carrying a large piece of meat is, somewhat surprisingly, technically known as 'humping') at Smithfield Market. They wear long white coats (sometimes hooded), beautifully besmirched with blood to look like abstract expressionist canvases and hump colossal carcasses on their backs.

In the market square of Harlow New Town (a cousin of Piccadilly as, like the InterContinental Hotel opposite, it was designed by Frederick Gibberd) there is a powerful statue of meat porters by Ralph Brown from 1959.

These – and the rather expensive porters at Heathrow – are the last vestiges of a profession that employed several thousand during the 17th–19th centuries. One would rent a porter as one might now order a courier bike or hire a man with a van. There were badge-wearing 'Ticket Porters' and 'Fellowship Porters' (who carried 'measurable' goods – salt, coal etc), both licensed by the City of London. William Darton illustrates the two sorts of porter (and a similar rest) in his *City Scenes* of 1828.

Porters needed energy and so drank quantities of beer and this gave rise to a brew called 'Porter'. The inns at this end of Piccadilly (on the edge of London) had porters' benches outside with 'boards' for depositing their loads. And, of course, they were used by breweries – as can be seen in William Hogarth's *Beer Street*.

I am not too fond of beer but during Lockdown I dreamed of being able to host some friends for martinis on this porters' board. It is a little high for a bar, but otherwise would provide a good vantage point from which to admire Piccadilly and Green Park.

← A licensed porter's badge, 1799

↑ William Darton shows a porter using a similar stand in his engraving of 1828

→ Ralph Brown's *Meat Porters* in Harlow New Town

↓ Two bummarees humping in Smithfield Market

57

Deputy Ranger's Lodge *1768*

To appreciate this entry you need to venture to the street in front of the French and Kuwaiti Embassies in Knightsbridge and to Thomas Cubitt's Albert Gate, which displays these two lovely 18th-century fallow deer. These deer originally decorated the entrance to the Deputy Ranger's Lodge in Green Park, across from Down Street, and were cast in the old sculpture yard in Engine Street (now Brick Street behind the Park Lane Hotel [*see* **34**]).

The lodge was built by Robert Adam in 1768 as the grace and favour home of the 'Deputy Ranger', a title bestowed by the Monarch on whomever was in favour at the time, following much jockeying by hopeful candidates. Lord William Gordon was the lucky recipient from 1778–1823. His daughter, Lady Frances Gordon, sat for Sir Joshua Reynolds' *Heads of Angels* in 1786–7 and lived in the lodge until her death in 1831. There seems to have been a tunnel linking this house to Coventry House on the other side of Piccadilly [**33**], also in large part by Adam. Could the tunnel have been an Adam-designed tunnel? That (perhaps with Etruscan ceiling decorations) must surely be the gift for the æsthete who has everything.

The house fell into disrepair, was demolished in 1841–2 and its plot incorporated into Green Park. Its address '150 Piccadilly' has been appropriated by the Hard Rock Café [**41**], whose correct address should be 137 Piccadilly. From Robert Adam to Adam and the Ants.

The deer seem content in their new Franco-Kuwaiti setting between Richard Seifert's Sheraton Park Tower Hotel and Hyde Park.

→ *Heads of Angels* by Sir Joshua Reynolds, for which Frances Gordon sat

↑ The deer in their original habitat

→ Adam's Deputy Ranger's Lodge

58 Gas Lights *c1900–50*

One of the great things about Green Park is that it does not shut at night. And so we quite often take a nocturnal stroll or find ourselves walking in darkness through the park back to Piccadilly from Victoria Station having returned from Glyndebourne or Gatwick.

To experience the park after dark is a wonderful thing as it is only lit by gas lights. To say 'lit' is incorrect as these lights illuminate nothing – rather they punctuate the park's walkways, like the lights on the runway of an exotic airport (on my first visit to Bamako, in the early 1990s, the runway was so dimly lit that a man was employed to blow a trumpet to clear the wildlife ahead of the 747-300 taking off).

There are 1,500 working gas lights left in London and a good number of them are in Green Park. They are now on timers but, together with all other London gas lights, are frequently adjusted by a team of four roaming British Gas engineers on scooters, with ladders strategically hidden around London.

The lights in Green Park comprise a whole range of models, ranging from the reigns of George IV to George VI, with some reproductions. They are a wonderful mix of size, design, age and components (an old lamp with a new shaft etc.) with all sorts of individual quirks, such as in the way the ladder rests are executed.

I will not seek to write about each model – much as I could probably quite easily become engrossed in lantern design – but here is a selection.

↑ The cypher of William IV

←↙↓ Leading lights: the variety adds grace and character to the park

←↑↗ The cyphers of Georges IV, V and VI

59 Green Park Underground Station 2012

GREEN PARK has the only underground station with a connection to William Kent (1685–1748). It was built in the late 1920s (replacing the station in Dover Street) in the corner of the new Devonshire House [19], which had replaced William Kent's original. The ticket office of the new station, however, occupied the wine cellar of the original house ('A bottle of Chablis with your Oyster Card, Madam?').

The station as it is now was built for the 2012 Olympic Games by architects Feilden+Mawson (and various others). While visually a bit busy, it is thoughtfully designed and well built. It uses roach stone (the variant of Portland stone containing fossils – also to be found on the Smithsons' Economist Building in St. James's Street), has a green copper roof roof (echoing the copper roofs of The Ritz above) and frames lovely views of Green Park. The roach stone features are repeated in a stylised way in a mural of giant fossil-like forms carved by John Maine of the Royal Academy (further up Piccadilly).

Outside are examples of Robin Day's wonderful Toro furniture, originally designed for London Transport in 1990.

The station is built into the hill and has a ramp leading into the park, providing a *post tenebras lux* moment for the weary underground traveller alighting at Green Park (a parkgoer's version of the experience one has when entering Oscar Niemeyer's wonderful Cathedral in Brasilia). It is also the only arched entrance into the park, a democratised reincarnation of the old Wellington Arch [54].

← The copper roof complements that of The Ritz behind

↓ Sniff, swirl, swipe: the wine cellar turned ticket hall

↑ John Maine's stylised fossil carvings

→ Light at the end of the Tube

↑ Toro seating by Robin Day, 1990

60

Water Fountains

A THREE-IN-ONE ENTRY for three water fountains of Green Park.

There has been a drinking fountain in a clearing on one of the northern walkways roughly opposite Down Street since 1860, when the architect Sydney Smirke (Robert Smirke's younger brother) designed an ornate three-basin affair.

By the 1950s it was falling apart and, in 1951, a competition was launched, supported by the Constance Fund (a charity to promote 'Ideal Sculpture' in parks and public places, started by the philanthropist and arts patron Constance Schweich in memory of her husband, fellow philanthropist and painter, Sigismund Goetze).

The competition was won by Estcourt J. Clack, sculptor of the Dickens Memorial on the Marylebone Road, and his – also three-basin – fountain was installed in 1952. The fountain (left) supports a statue of Diana of the Treetops. Other contestants included Maurice Lambert, Harold J. Dow (who went on to do the reliefs at 89 Piccadilly [*see* 24]) and Siegfried Charoux. The statue was moved in 2011 to its current position at the park entrance to the Underground [59] to give a focal point to the new scheme.

The abstract composition *Watering Holes*, by Robin Monotti Architects and Mark Titman, was installed in its place in 2014. It was donated by The Tiffany & Co. Foundation as part of a gift to restore and renew the drinking fountains across all the Royal Parks. This fountain also incorporates the three-basin composition, albeit vertically.

The Royal Parks describe the 2014 fountain as 'Art-Led' and I think that is why I have always found it difficult: having a Barbara Hepworth-esque sculpture is one thing; having one with buttons to sprinkle water into one's mouth is quite another (although it would be amusing to apply this principle to other sculptors – imagine a refreshing/rejuvenating sip at the bosom of a Henry Moore *Mother and Child*). The Diana fountain, while a little too sweet for my taste, keeps art and hydration separate – a much better solution.

↑ *Watering Holes* by Monotti and Titman

↓ An early 20TH century postcard showing Sydney Smirke's 1860 design

→ Estcourt J. Clack's *Dickens Memorial* featuring characters from the author's principal novels

61 The Temple of Peace 1749

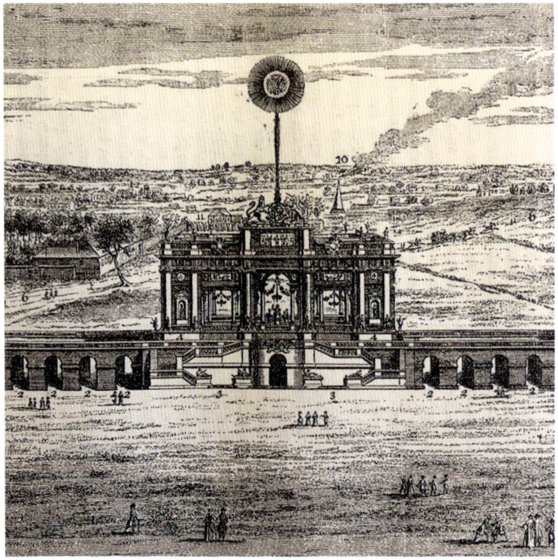

GREEN PARK has two main artistic legacies – Georg Friedrich Händel's *Music for the Royal Fireworks* and the birth of Auto-Destructive Art, 200 years before Gustav Metzger, John Latham and Jean Tinguely.

It all came about in 1749 with the publication of the *Treaty of Aix-la-Chapelle* at the end of the War of the Austrian Succession when George II decided to have a fireworks party on a colossal scale. He engaged Italian designers (led by a Signor Servandoni, designer of international parties and who also worked on parts of Saint-Sulpice in Paris) and pyrotechnicians (Messrs Ruggieri & Sarti of Bologna under the direction of Captain Thomas Desaguliers, Chief Firemaster of His Majesty's Laboratory) and, for the music, Händel, then living in Brook Street in the house that Jimi Hendrix went on to occupy in the 1960s.

The launchpad for the pyrotechnic display was to be 'The Temple of Peace', a structure 400 ft long and 114 ft high accommodating musicians below a huge allegory of Peace attended by Neptune and Mars, above which George II would be shown in bas relief bestowing peace on a most grateful Britannia. And high above that would burn a huge and magnificent Sun.

Händel set about composing suitable music, starting with a military overture incorporating 100 cannons being fired from the Temple's arcades, and representing a stormy sea suddenly subsiding into calm. The orchestra would comprise 40 trumpets, 20 French horns, 16 hautboys, 12 side drums and 8 kettle drums (but, on the King's strict instructions and against Händel's will, 'no fiddles'). The fireworks numbered around 30,000.

On the evening of 27 April 1749, The King and his guests, members of the Houses of Lords and Commons and the Privy Council took their places in specially-built pavilions, with thousands of other spectators thronging into the park. The cannons were fired and, as Händel's overture began, part of The Temple of Peace caught fire leading to a huge conflagration and explosions amid scenes of extreme distress, panic and chaos, with the wounded being rushed to The Lanesborough Hotel (at the time St. George's Hospital).

How peaceful it all seems now.

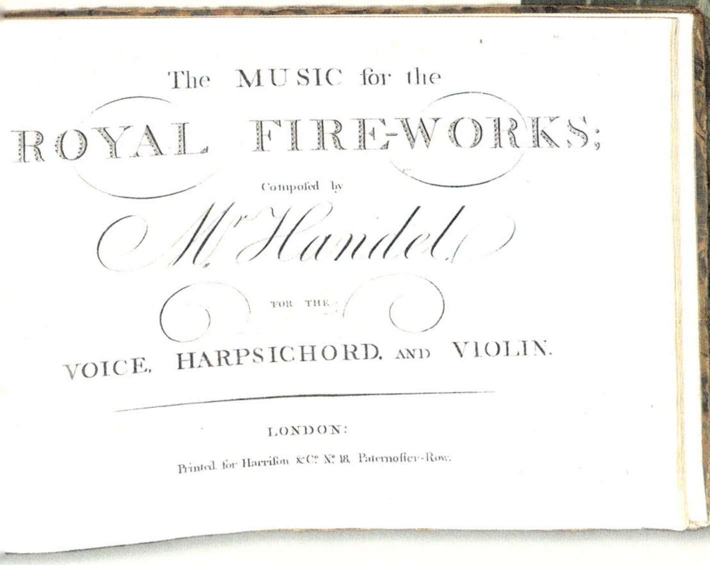

← The first edition of the score

↑ The intended effect

↑ Händel's music and Green Park have become indissociable

← Servandoni's design for the Temple and Machine

62

Queen Caroline's Library 1737

CAROLINE WAS a most intellectual Queen. As a newcomer from Germany, she brought with her the culture of the courts of Dresden, Brandenburg and Hanover and was also determined to integrate herself (and George II) into the British monarchy (and to master the English language). The library she had built in the southeastern corner of Green Park (near St. James's Palace) epitomises these traits.

In 1727 Caroline commissioned her favourite architect, William Kent, to build the library and it was completed only a month before her death in 1737. The library housed her wonderfully cosmopolitan and wide-ranging collection of books, with publications from all over Europe, in particular contemporary works in French (47%), English (35%), Italian, German and Latin, bringing new life to the rather neglected tradition of British Royal libraries. (Both she and George were enthusiastic bibliophiles and readers. While George kept a private library in Hanover, 'both she and the King always read in bed both after dinner & after Supper' according to her friend Lady Suffolk.)

Caroline commissioned Michael Rysbrack to produce a series of 11 terracotta and marble *bustos* of British monarchs from William the Conqueror to George II and herself to decorate the library. Only three of the terracottas survive and these are now at Windsor Castle: Edward the Black Prince, Edward VI and Elizabeth I.

George continued to expand the collection after Caroline died but it was dispersed after his death. The library was damaged in the fire that engulfed the Temple of Peace in 1749 [61] and by 1790 was being used as a store room. The building was briefly used by the Duke of York as his library (1815–25) and then demolished to make way for his new residence, Lancaster House [1].

Caroline truly is the Queen of Green Park (or Upper St. James's Park as it was then known). She embellished the park before it was fashionable, adding, not only her library, but also the reservoir/lake (filled in during the 19th century) and the Queen's Walk (which we have already explored [see 1–17]). That is why I dedicated this book to her.

← The library (middle building with the blank upper story) around 1800, with Westminster Abbey in the background

↑ The surviving terracotta bust of Edward VI. The set of busts can be seen in the image of the interior opposite

↓ The reservoir/lake, another of Queen Caroline's creations *(see pages 6–7 for full image)*

63 Temple of Concord 1814

THE END of the Napoleonic Wars and the centenary of the accession to the throne of the Hanoverian monarchs called for another big party. In 1814 the Prince Regent invited all the 'Top People of Victorious Europe' to London [*see also* **32** *and* **34**] where they were treated to an array of spectacles, among which a pyrotechnic display of magnificent proportions in Green Park, as well as the Sinofication of St. James's Park (culminating in a Chinese bridge over the lake – then the Canal – topped with a seven-storey pagoda designed by John Nash), displays of hot air balloon ascents and naumachia on the Serpentine.

A large area of Green Park was taken over by a huge revolving mock castle designed by Sir William Congreve. After several hours of fireworks, at midnight on 1 August 1814 (the anniversary of the Battle of the Nile), amid specially created smoke and further grandiose fireworks, the revolving fortress (shown on the left) miraculously morphed into The Temple of Concord (shown on the right).

This time there were no mishaps, at least in Green Park. In St. James's Park, however, things had gone less smoothly. The pagoda, as planned, spewed forth fireworks from each of its gas-lit storeys, but then began vigorously to sway and to smoke before bursting into flames and crashing into the Canal. And, sure enough, a few months later Napoléon escaped from Elba and the Napoleonic wars resumed.

Averse as I am to filling our parks with monuments, I have always dreamed of erecting a new Temple of Concorde – a celebration of our most beautiful and beloved passenger æroplane of the 20TH century, similarly revolving (rapidly) on a pyrotechnically-lit stand. Perhaps to keep poor old Marble Arch company.

→ Pride before the fall: The Temple of Concord is unveiled while behind, in St. James's Park, pyrotechnics begin at the Chinese Pagoda

↑ Nash's Chinese Pagoda, before it crashed into the lake

→ Naumachia on the Serpentine: the Battle of the Nile re-enacted

64

The Pantheon 1913

I HAVE NOT attempted to write about the landscaping and the trees of Green Park but will make an exception for what is Green Park's most enigmatic place – part wood, part monument, part structure: The Pantheon, as we shall call it, a perfect circle of trees with a diameter (43 metres) exactly that of the Pantheon in Rome (I am neither technical nor athletic enough to have measured its height but it feels right too), creating a grand yet intimate and secluded domed space with the assembled canopies of the trees leaving a perfect oculus through which to admire a piece of sky.

The Pantheon is beautifully positioned in front of the three loveliest (and classical or classical in spirit) buildings on Green Park: Spencer House [7] and, either side, Bridgewater House and 26 St. James's Place [5 *and* 8]. The façade of Spencer House with its oversized pediment almost recreates the portico of the Roman Pantheon.

No one knows much about this place other than the bare essentials: there was once a bandstand here (erected in 1906 and demolished in the 1970s or 1980s) and the trees were planted in 1913 and can be seen on the Ordinance Survey map of 1916 and in several 1920s aerial views.

One aspect is fundamentally different to the Roman Pantheon, however. There are 13 trees – which I do not think corresponds to anything in the Pantheon (where the magic number is 28, a 'perfect number'). And this is where a conversation with an elegantly spiritual Indian lady and her friend encountered in the Park Pantheon one Sunday afternoon opened a whole new world... For many this place has an ancient spiritual meaning: 'It felt like I'd entered a different dimension... I counted the trees ... yes there were 13. One for each of the Celtic, lunar months of the year. Whoa. Spooky. What was this? A Druidic grove in the middle of Green Park?' writes Chris Street on *earthstars.co.uk*. Many think that this place bristles with 'ley-lines'.

And that is the charm of Green Park – for some it is Verona while for others it is Sedona. A place that is big and generous and full of whatever meaning the wanderer wishes to impose on it.

→ The old bandstand is visible with the trees not yet mature in this 1928 image

↓ 1916 Ordnance Survey map showing the trees and the bandstand

↑ The Pantheon with Spencer House in the background

↓ Giovanni Paolo Panini, *Interior of the Pantheon, Rome,* c.1734

65 The End of Green Park

GREEN PARK has been the subject of all manner of intrusion and reduction over the centuries. George II and Queen Caroline erected various (excellent) structures in the 18TH century [62] (and George almost burnt the whole place down with one of them [61]) and, in 1767, George III appropriated around a quarter of the park when creating the gardens for Buckingham Palace (as can be seen if one compares the maps on the front and back endpapers). The past 60 years have been particularly cruel: first in 1961, when Hyde Park Corner was turned into a roundabout, thereby detaching the Wellington Arch from the park and using a large slice of the park for the roundabout ([46] and [54]); and then in the early 2000s, when the remains of that end of the park were ruined first by the addition of a huge bicycle rental stand and then by the installation of the terrible Bomber Command Memorial [55].

But true disaster loomed when, in the early 19TH century, the great Sir John Soane prepared plans for the then Prince Regent to convert Green Park into a new royal palace as an alternative to the restoration and enlargement of Buckingham House. Happily, George IV ended up going with John Nash and a reworking of Buckingham House into Buckingham Palace and the threatened catastrophe was averted.

While the world would have gained a magnificent new work by Soane, the new palace would have been the end of Green Park.

• • •

And so it is time for me to end my wanderings around Green Park. Thank you for joining me. If you have read this from the comfort of an armchair please come and see the real thing (again or for the first time) – what my notes have not sought to convey is just how incredibly lovely, engaging and varied our little park is, before one even starts to look at its surrounding buildings, monuments and structures.
— Piccadilly, June 2020

↓ A contemporary image of Sir John Soane's proposed scheme to replace Buckingham House with a new Royal palace on the site of Green Park. The project did not receive Royal approval, saving the park for our times

↑ The view east along Piccadilly from Hyde Park Corner, c.1810. On the left, Apsley House **[47]** with its original Adam brothers design

Bibliography

Adcock. St. J. Ed. (1926). *Wonderful London; The World's Greatest City Described by its Best Writers and Pictured by its Finest Photographers*. London: The Fleetway House

Anonymous. (1883). *Handbook of the Jones Collection in the South Kensington Museum*. London: Chapman and Hall, Limited

Anonymous. (c. 1925). *The League of Nations; A Pictorial Survey*. Geneva: League of Nations

Anonymous. (1980). *Selwyn House, St. James's, London: A short history of Selwyn House from 1600 to the present day*. St. Helens: Pilkington Brothers Limited

Anonymous. (1950). *A Short History of Selwyn House and its site; St. James's London 1543–1949*. St. Helens: Pilkington Brothers Limited

Beresford Chancellor, E. (1909). *Wanderings in Piccadilly, Mayfair and Pall Mall*. London: Ward & Co

Besant, W. (1909). *London in the Nineteenth Century*. London: Adam & Charles Black

Binney, M. (1999). *The Ritz Hotel, London*. London: Thames & Hudson

Bowdler, R.H. and S.P. Brindle. (2015). *Wellington Arch, Marble Arch and Six Great War Memorials*. London: English Heritage

Bradbury, O. (2008). *The Lost Mansions of Mayfair*. London: Historical Publications

Bradley, S. and N. Pevsner. (2003). *London 6: Westminster*. New Haven and London: Yale University Press

Braybrooke, N. (1959). *London Green: The Story of Kensington Gardens, Hyde Park, Green Park, St. James's Park*. London: Victor Gollancz Ltd

Britainfromabove.org.uk [accessed 14 June 2020]

Carverhill, G. (2018). *The Rootes Story. Volume I: The Making of a Global Automotive Empire*. Marlborough: The Crowood Press

Clogg, R. (2016). *Frederick North, The Fifth Earl of Guildford (1766–1827): The Philhellene's Philhellene*. Available on *albertcohen.gr* [accessed 14 June 2020]

Colby, R. (1966). *Mayfair: A Town within London*. London: Country Life Limited

Cooper, N. (2011). *The Photography of Bedford Lemere & Co*. Swindon: English Heritage

Cornforth, J. (2000). *London Interiors from the Archives of Country Life*. London: Aurum Press Limited

Curtis, W.J.R. (1994). *Denys Lasdun: Architecture, City, Landscape*. London: Phaidon

Darton, W. (1828). *City Scenes. Or a Peep into London*. London: Harvey and Darton. Available at *gutenberg.org* [accessed 14 June 2020]

Dasent, A. (1920). *Piccadilly in Three Centuries*. London: Macmillan and Co, Limited

Davies, P. (2009). *Lost London 1870–1945*. Croxley Green: Transatlantic Press

Defoe, D. (1929). *A tour thro' London about the year 1725*. London: B.T. Batsford

Denby, E. (1998). *Grand Hotels: reality and illusion: an architectural and social history*. London: Reaktion Books

↓ Improvements at Hyde Park Corner and the removal of the Wellington statue **[*see* 54]**, 1883

Dutton, R. (1952). *London Homes*. London: Allan Wingate

Fuller, S. (1971). *144 Piccadilly*. New York: Richard W. Baron Publishing Co, Inc.

Girling, B. (1996). *Images of London: City of Westminster*. Stroud: Tempus Publishing

Graves, C. (1964). *Leather Armchairs: A guide to the Great Clubs of London*. New York: Coward-McCann, Inc.

Inwood, S. (2005). *City of Cities: The Birth of Modern London*. London: Macmillan

Jay, E. (2006). 'Queen Caroline's Library and its European Contexts'. *Book History* 9, 31–55. Available at muse.jhu.edu [accessed 14 June 2020]

Larwood, J. (1870). *The Story of the London Parks*. London: John Camden Hotten

Lees-Milne, J. (2008). *Diaries*. London: John Murray

Lejeune, A. and M. Lewis. (1984). *The Gentlemen's Clubs of London*. London: Parkgate Books Ltd

Macqueen-Pope, W. (1960). *Goodbye Piccadilly*. London: Michael Joseph Ltd

Rabbitts, P. (2014). *London's Royal Parks*. Oxford: Shire Publications

Regencyhistory.com [accessed 14 June 2020]

↑ Claude Monet's painting of Green Park, c.1870, with the Wellington statue visible in the distance still in place atop the Arch **[54]**

Richardson, A.E. and C. Lovett Gill. (1911). *London Houses from 1660 to 1820; A consideration of their Architecture and Detail*. London: B.T. Batsford

Royal Parks, The. *Ed.* (1997). *Buildings and Monuments in the Royal Parks*. London: The Royal Parks

Shappard, F.H.W. (1960). *Survey of London: Volumes 29 and 30, St. James's Westminster Part 1*. London: London County Council. Available at *british-history.ac.uk* [accessed 14 June 2020]

Smith, J.T. (1849). *The Streets of London*. London: Richard Bentley

Stamp, G. (2013). *Anti Ugly: Excursions in English Architecture and Design*. London: Aurum Press Ltd

Street, G.S. (1907). *The Ghosts of Piccadilly*. London: Constable and Company Ltd

Ude, L.E. (1829). *The French Cook*. London: John Ebers and Co.

Walford, E. (1878). *Old and New London: A Narrative of its History, its People, and its Places. Volume 4, Westminster and the Western Suburbs*. London, Paris & New York: Cassell Petter & Galpin.

Wheatley, H.B. (1891). *London, Past and Present: Its History, Associations and Traditions*. London: John Murray

——— (1870). *Round About Piccadilly and Pall Mall; Or, a Ramble from Haymarket to Hyde Park Consisting of a Retrospect of the Various Changes That Have Occurred in the Court End of London*. London: Smith, Elder & Co

Williams, G. (1978). *The Royal Parks of London*. London: Constable and Company Ltd

Wodehouse, P.G. (1918). *Piccadilly Jim*. London: Herbert Jenkins Limited

Index

↑ Hatchett's Hotel, Coffee House and White Horse Cellar on Piccadilly, founded in 1753, starting point for the mail coaches

↓ Queen Victoria's Diamond Jubilee, Piccadilly, 1897

← Mournings of Green Park: George V's funeral procession, 1936

↓ Mantras of Green Park: Hare Krishna procession, 2018

↓ Naked aggression: a cannonball outside the Cavalry and Guards Club **[38]**

← Naked cycling: the annual parade, 2016

← His Grace The Duke of Queensberry sitting on his balcony in Piccadilly **[42]**

Image credits

All photographs are the author's own except where noted below; prints, postcards and other illustrative material are in the author's collection except where noted below.

Credits refer to the images reading clockwise from upper left.

Full details of books can be found in the bibliography

• • •

COVER
© Laura Hodgson

ENDPAPERS
Images courtesy of Daniel Crouch Rare Books *crouchrarebooks.com*

DEDICATION
Royal Collections Trust/© Her Majesty Queen Elizabeth II 2020

PREFACE
© Tate, photo © Tate

PART I
p.18: Adcock, *Wonderful London*

[1] Wikimedia Commons; Keystone Press/Alamy Photo; PA Images/Alamy Stock Photo

[2] © National Portrait Gallery, London; Yale Center for British Art, Paul Mellon Fund, B2014.2

[4] John Maltby/RIBA Collections; *A Short History of Selwyn House*, Courtesy of Pilkington Group Limited

[8] Courtesy of *architecture-history.org*

[9] © National Trust Images; © National Portrait Gallery, London; Survey of London/ Bartlett School of Architecture, UCL

[10] Courtesy of The National Gallery of Art, Washington, Gift of the 50TH Anniversary Gift Committee

[11] Wikimedia Commons; Waddesdon Image Library, John Webb

[12] Walford, *Old and New London*; Wikimedia Commons; The RIBA Collections; Survey of London/Bartlett School of Architecture, UCL

[13] Wikimedia Commons; GRANGER; Michael Stroud/ Hulton Archive via Getty Images

[14] Country Life Picture Library (2)

[15] © Laura Hodgson; Ude, *The French Cook*

[16] Government Art Collection, Department for Digital, Culture, Media and Sport; *The Illustrated London News*, 1919; Courtesy of The Ritz Hotel

[17] John F. Stephenson/ Hulton Royals Collection via Getty Images

[18] *ianvisits.co.uk*; Isabella Stewart Gardner Museum, Boston [Detail]; Wikimedia Commons, photo by Minky69

[19] Walford, *Old and New London*; Country Life Picture Library (2)

[20] Richardson and Lovett, *London Houses*; Look and Learn; Grace's Guide to British Industrial History

[21] Wikimedia Commons; © National Portrait Gallery, London

[22] City of London, Metropolitan Archives (Collage: the London Picture Archive, 135770); *idem* (138218); Martin's Bank Archive

[23] Walford, *Old and New London*; City of London Metropolitan Archives (SC/PHL/ OL/0999)

[24] Wikimedia Commons; Colin Westwood/RIBA Collections

[25] City of London, Metropolitan Archives (Collage: the London Picture Archive, 137428)

[27] Bedford Lemere & Co/Alamy Stock Photo; Westminster City Archives CACCCD1318/ Incident Number 828 (p.28); © George Jaworskyj

[28] Historic England Archive; Wikimedia Commons; Anon., *Handbook of The Jones Collection*

↓ Bird watching 1967: The Rolling Stones soaking up local glamour in front of the Queen's Walk

↑ Art meets nature on the railings of Green Park, c.1965

[29] Historic England Archive

[32] © National Portrait Gallery, London; Country Life Picture Library; Chronicle/Alamy Stock Photo; Besant, *London in the Nineteenth Century*

[33] © National Portrait Gallery, London; Wikimedia Commons/ United States Library of Congress (pga 14088)

[34] Courtesy of Sheraton Grand Hotel

[35] Courtesy of Athenaeum Hotel; Architectural Press Archive/RIBA

[36] Anon., *The League of Nations: A Pictorial Survey;* Wikimedia Commons, photo by Andrew Gray

[37] © The Trustees of the British Museum. All rights reserved; Royal Automobile Club (Archive)

[39] Architectural Press Archive/RIBA Collections (2)

[40] Wikimedia Commons; Royal Collections Trust/© Her Majesty Queen Elizabeth II 2020; Nicolas Breach/RIBA Collections

[42] Yale Center for British Art, Paul Mellon Collection

[43] Wikimedia Commons, from *Vanity Fair* magazine dated June 17, 1871; Collection: Portsmouth Museums and Visitor Services; Wikimedia Commons (2)

[44] Wikimedia Commons, originally published in *The Equinox* volume 1, issue 10 (1913)

[45] Keystone Press/Alamy Stock Photo; City of London, Metropolitan Archives (Collage: the London Picture Archive, 13851); Wikimedia Commons

[46] City of London, Metropolitan Archives (Collage: the London Picture Archive, 138243); Courtesy of Bishopsgate Institute; Adam 51/68: Sir John Soane's Museum, London. Photograph by Ardon Bar Hama

[47] Defoe, *A Tour thro' London about the year 1725*

[48] Google Maps

PART II

p.116: Adcock, *Wonderful London*

[49] © Victoria and Albert Museum, London; Album/ Alamy Stock Photos; © Laura Hodgson

[53] Courtesy of A.H. Baldwin & Sons Ltd.

[54] Wikimedia Commons (4)

[56] Darton, *City Scenes;* © Museum of London; © Ken Griffiths; Courtesy of the Estate of Ralph Brown/Pangolin London

[57] Collection: Denver Art Museum; Digital Library for the Decorative Arts and Material Culture, University of Wisconsin; Larwood, *The Story of London Parks*

[60] © Laura Hodgson

[61] Walford, *Old and New London*; The Buccleuch Collections; The Foundling Museum, Gerald Coke Handel Collection; © Victoria and Albert Museum, London. Given by the Rev. R. Brooke

[62] Album/Alamy Stock Photo; Royal Collections Trust/© Her Majesty Queen Elizabeth II 2020 (2)

[63] 'The fortress (which inclosed *(sic)* the Grand Pavillion) in the Green Park, with the ascent of the balloon' (1814). *Prints, Drawings and Watercolors from the Anne S.K. Brown Military Collection*. Brown Digital Repository. Brown University Library. *https://repository.library.brown.edu/studio/item/bdr:228331/*; British Library; © The Trustees of the British Museum. All rights reserved; Look and Learn/Peter Jackson Collection; THE MET museum, Gift of Gray Foy, 2013

[64] © Historic England; Courtesy National Gallery of Art, Washington

[65] P93: Sir John Soane's Museum, London

BIBLIOGRAPHY

p.152: Wikimedia Commons
p.154: Wikimedia Commons
p.155: Wikimedia Commons/ Philadelphia Museum of Art, Purchased with the W. P. Wilstach Fund, 1921

INDEX

p.158: Album/Alamy Stock Photo

IMAGE CREDITS

p.165: Trinity Mirror/Mirrorpix/ Alamy Stock Photo
p.166: akg-images/A.F.Kersting (Painter(s) unknown)
p.167: © Laura Hodgson

ABOUT THE AUTHOR

Andrew Jones has lived on Piccadilly for over 15 years, using it as a base for his travels around the world and Green Park. An international lawyer by profession, Andrew collects Modern British art and design. He has written for *Blueprint* magazine, *Drawing Matter, The London Gardener, The Financial Times* and *The World of Interiors*; served on the awards committee for Masterpiece London art fair; and sits on the board of Save Venice Inc.

OXFORD STREET
Portman Square
Manchester Square
Cavendish Square
Hanover Square
Grosvenor Square
Berkeley Square
Soho Sq.
Golden Square
St. James's Square
Leicester Square
HYDE PARK
The Ring
Reservoir
Serpentine River
THE KINGS PRIVATE ROAD
Cumberland Gate
Grosvenor Gate
Statue
Hyde Park Corner
PICCADILLY
GREEN PARK
Constitution Hill
KINGS GARDEN
Kings Palace
ST. JAMES'S PARK
PALL MALL
The Mall
Bird Cage Walk
Horse Guards Parade
Treasury
Admiralty
WHITEHALL
Charing Cross
Regent St.
Haymarket
Quadrant
Brook Street
Grosvenor Street
Bond Street
Piccadilly
KNIGHTSBRIDGE
Lowndes Square
Belgrave Square
Eaton Square
Eccleston Square
Wilton Cres.
Sloane Street
Sloane Sq.
Chelsea Road
Kings Road
Willow Walk
Vauxhall Bridge Road
Horse Ferry Road
Tothill Str.
Orchard Street
Brompton
Montpelier Squ.
Trevor Sq.
Alexander Sq.
Onslow
Rutland Ho.
Hans Place
Cadogan Place
Royal Military Asylum
Chelsea Water Works
Vincent Sq.
Westminster Abbey
WESTMINSTER